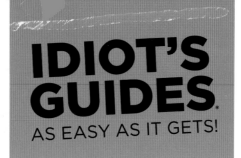

Playing
Guitar

ABERDEENSHIRE LIBRARIES	
3115096	
Bertrams	04/09/2013
787.871	£12.99

by David Hodge

Aberdeenshire

This book is dedicated to the memory of Thomas "Todd" Lange.

ALPHA BOOKS

Published by Penguin Group (USA) Inc.

Penguin Group (USA) Inc., 375 Hudson Street, New York, New York 10014, USA • Penguin Group (Canada), 90 Eglinton Avenue East, Suite 700, Toronto, Ontario M4P 2Y3, Canada (a division of Pearson Penguin Canada Inc.) • Penguin Books Ltd., 80 Strand, London WC2R 0RL, England • Penguin Ireland, 25 St. Stephen's Green, Dublin 2, Ireland (a division of Penguin Books Ltd.) • Penguin Group (Australia), 250 Camberwell Road, Camberwell, Victoria 3124, Australia (a division of Pearson Australia Group Pty. Ltd.) • Penguin Books India Pvt. Ltd., 11 Community Centre, Panchsheel Park, New Delhi—110 017, India • Penguin Group (NZ), 67 Apollo Drive, Rosedale, North Shore, Auckland 1311, New Zealand (a division of Pearson New Zealand Ltd.) • Penguin Books (South Africa) (Pty.) Ltd., 24 Sturdee Avenue, Rosebank, Johannesburg 2196, South Africa • Penguin Books Ltd., Registered Offices: 80 Strand, London WC2R 0RL, England

International Standard Book Number: 978-1-61564-417-9
Library of Congress Catalog Card Number: 2013935162

15 14 13   8 7 6 5 4 3 2 1

Interpretation of the printing code: The rightmost number of the first series of numbers is the year of the book's printing; the rightmost number of the second series of numbers is the number of the book's printing. For example, a printing code of 13-1 shows that the first printing occurred in 2013.

Note: This publication contains the opinions and ideas of its author. It is intended to provide helpful and informative material on the subject matter covered. It is sold with the understanding that the author and publisher are not engaged in rendering professional services in the book. If the reader requires personal assistance or advice, a competent professional should be consulted. The author and publisher specifically disclaim any responsibility for any liability, loss, or risk, personal or otherwise, which is incurred as a consequence, directly or indirectly, of the use and application of any of the contents of this book.

Most Alpha books are available at special quantity discounts for bulk purchases for sales promotions, premiums, fundraising, or educational use. Special books, or book excerpts, can also be created to fit specific needs. For details, write: Special Markets, Alpha Books, 375 Hudson Street, New York, NY 10014.

Trademarks: All terms mentioned in this book that are known to be or are suspected of being trademarks or service marks have been appropriately capitalized. Alpha Books and Penguin Group (USA) Inc. cannot attest to the accuracy of this information. Use of a term in this book should not be regarded as affecting the validity of any trademark or service mark.

Publisher: Mike Sanders

Executive Managing Editor: Billy Fields

Senior Acquisitions Editor: Tom Stevens

Development Editor: John Etchison

Senior Production Editor/Proofreader: Janette Lynn

Photographer: Ogden Gigli

Book Designer: Brian Massey

Cover Designer: William Thomas

Indexer: Johnna VanHoose Dinse

ALWAYS LEARNING   PEARSON

Contents

Contents

Appendixes

Introduction

Making music on the guitar may seem nothing short of magical to you. Guitarists seem to create emotions out of sound when they play—the harplike notes of a lullaby; the sad bending notes of a blues song; the pulsing, hard-edged drive of a rock anthem; or the cocky twang of a country tune.

Whatever kind of music you enjoy, you can play it on a guitar. You can strum chords to sing over. You can fingerpick mesmerizing melodies and harmonies and bass lines. You can beat out exciting dance rhythms with your fingertips.

Learning to play the guitar is not hard. The basics of playing are the same no matter what type of guitar you have or what type of music you want to play. You don't even have to be able to read music.

Idiot's Guide: Playing Guitar is designed to get you started playing guitar right away, even if you've never even held a guitar before. You'll get a thorough step-by-step rundown of all the fundamentals of playing, and then learn to expand on those basic skills with more intermediate guitar techniques.

If you've always wanted to learn to play the guitar, then get ready to make some magic.

Get ready to make some music!

How This Book Is Organized

This book is divided into five parts:

Part 1, Getting Your Gear, introduces you to the guitar and helps you understand which one might be best for you—at least as a first guitar! You'll also learn to change your guitar's strings and some basic maintenance tips.

Part 2, Warming Up to Play, teaches you how to tune your guitar as well as how to hold it properly to get the best playing out of both your left and right hand.

Part 3, Getting Good with Rhythm, gives you a solid foundation in the basics of making, strumming, and changing chords.

Part 4, Growing Beyond the Beginner Stage, builds on the skills you picked up in Part 3. Here you'll get introduced to playing half-barre chords and different styles of fingerpicking in addition to left-hand slurring techniques such as hammer-ons and pull-offs. Your guitar playing will take a huge leap forward.

Part 5, Adding Theory to Your Playing, helps you take your skills even further. You'll learn about using capos and transposing, explore different guitar tunings, and discover some alternative picking styles.

Introduction

You'll also find that almost every topic in Parts 3, 4, and 5 contains numerous musical examples and exercises, all designed specifically for this book to help you learn quickly and easily. Plus you'll get a number of songs that serve as examples for the different ideas and techniques you read about. In fact, all the songs incorporate parts of the accompanying exercise as part of the arrangement. You'll find these bits taken from the exercises color-coded into the music of the songs.

Due to copyright issues, all the songs you'll find in *Idiot's Guide: Playing Guitar* are traditional songs in the public domain. But each song has also been arranged specifically for this book in order to create fun, musically interesting pieces for you to play and enjoy.

But Wait! There's More!

Throughout this book you'll find songs and exercises with links to online audio tracks. Wherever you see the headphones icon, point your browser to idiotsguides.com/playingguitar, click on the appropriate track, and listen to the sample exactly as it should be played!

All these recordings have been produced professionally in a studio in order to give them the best possible audio quality. Thanks to Todd Mack and Will Curtiss of Off the Beat-n-Track Studio in Sheffield, Massachusetts, for recording, mixing, and mastering the audio; and special thanks to my good friend Nick Torres for his great singing on many of these songs.

Acknowledgments

As always, my first thanks go to my terrific agent, Marilyn Allen, for thinking of me when this project came up.

A huge thank you to the team at Alpha Books, with special acknowledgment to Tom Stevens and John Etchison, and especially to Brian Massey, who created the art design and whose ideas have shaped this book's tutorial philosophy.

The exceptionally precise and clean photographs for the chord fingerings, as well as most of the other photos, are the work of photographer Ogden Gigli (www.ogdengigli.com), for whom there is not enough praise. Ogden pulled off the almost impossible task of recreating images from the guitarist's perspective and made this book even better than we all thought possible.

I also would like to thank John Reichert for use of his photo on the "Playing in a Group" pages.

Finally, as always, I have to thank the people who do so much to inspire and motivate me on a daily basis: Paul Hackett, the creator of Guitar Noise (www.guitarnoise.com); my youngest brother, Tom; and my great friends Laura Pager and Greg Nease, whose hands also are literally all over this book—that's him posing for all the chord charts and fretboard photos.

And to Karen Berger (who took the photo for Part 1 and Gene Autry's guitar), no amount of thanks will ever be enough. Fortunately, I have a lifetime to keep giving them to you.

Part 1

Getting Your Gear

There are seemingly almost as many different guitars as there are songs to play. It's easy to get a bit overwhelmed trying to decide which instrument would be best for you to start with.

For most beginners, it's not even a question of brands or manufacturers but whether to get an acoustic, a classical, or an electric guitar. It comes down to a simple question:

Which guitar is going to make you want to play it day after day?

In this section, you'll get a rundown on each of these three types of guitars, plus some tips on how to find the one that's right for you.

The Guitar—Past and Present

Today's guitars come from a very long family tree, dating back beyond the Scandinavian lutes and the Arabic ouds of the eighth century. During the Renaissance, guitars were much smaller, with very thin necks sporting eight to ten gut strings, usually set in pairs, or "courses." Still, just as today, they were both strummed to provide rhythmic accompaniment and plucked to create musical melodies.

In the 1800s, guitars began to look a lot more recognizable as guitars, with six strings and larger bodies. The designs of Antonio de Torres, in particular, led to the instrument we call the modern-day classical guitar.

While Torres was creating guitars in his native Spain, Christian Frederick Martin was designing and building guitars in Nazareth, Pennsylvania. And in the 1890s, Orville Gibson, who had no formal luthier training, manufactured guitars at his home workshop in Kalamazoo, Michigan.

The strength of these American designers' guitars proved to be a match made in heaven for the steel strings that were being introduced to the world at the turn of the twentieth century.

This Panormo from 1836 shares many similarities with today's classical guitars.

This 1950's steel-string acoustic guitar was played by legendary American folk singer Gene Autry.

The Three Types of Guitars

Most guitars can be put into one of three distinct categories: *classical*, *acoustic*, and *electric*. There are, of course, exceptions, not to mention many different subcategories within each type.

It's important to note here that you can play almost any kind of music on any kind of guitar. You just have to know that the music you make is going to sound different depending on the guitar you use to play it.

Classical guitars have nylon strings and are used to play classical music or flamenco music (there are flamenco guitars, too, which are smaller, lighter versions of the classical). But you'll also hear them in many other musical genres, such as jazz and Latin music.

Acoustic or steel-string guitars are far and away the most popular of guitars, and there isn't a musical genre in which you won't hear someone playing one. While classical guitars are almost all identical in overall appearance and shape, acoustic guitars come in many different subcategories.

Classical   Acoustic   Electric

Electric guitars are the brash kids of the family. They come in two main types: solid body and hollow (or semi-hollow) body. It's impossible to think of music without electric guitars. You'll hear them in rock, blues, jazz, country, and just about any other type of music you can think of. Electric guitars usually have very narrow fingerboards, and the strings are much lighter than those of an acoustic.

It's a common debate among guitarists as to whether it's best to learn on a classical, an acoustic, or an electric, and there are good arguments for each type of guitar. Ultimately, though, you should figure out what kind of guitar will make you happy, excited, and eager to play every day, through the good, the getting better, and the great days of practicing ahead of you. If you think you've made a bad choice of guitars, then you're not going to play it, and that would be a shame—not to mention a waste of a good guitar.

Plus, remember that your first guitar is very probably going to be just that—the first of many you'll play and enjoy throughout your lifetime.

Getting Your Guitar

Just as people choose to play the guitar for many reasons, there are all sorts of guitars to choose from. If you think there's only one "right" guitar for you, you might miss out on many that will make beautiful music with you.

You want a guitar to fit you like a shoe does (or should!). Many people assume that they can just sit down and play any guitar, but beginners have to take a lot of things into account. The first is comfort. You may never have played a guitar before. You may never have held a guitar before. But you certainly know what it's like to be uncomfortable—and you really want to play attention to that when you're trying out guitars.

This is even more important if you're planning to buy a guitar online. If you've never tried to even hold a guitar before, you could end up ordering something that you cannot play, and instead of looking at other guitars you might just give up the instrument. You owe it to yourself to get your hands on as many different types of guitars as you can, just to see what works for you in terms of the instrument's size and shape.

Make sure you can both stand and sit comfortably with the guitar. Can you easily reach the frets of the neck with the fingertips of your left hand? Is the neck smooth, or can you feel sharp edges of the frets as you slide your hand along? While sitting, can you strum and pick the strings with your right hand without making your right arm uncomfortable?

If at all possible, bring a friend who plays guitar along with you when you shop. Initially, you want to try out whichever instruments strike your fancy. If you are able to pare down your choices to a handful, then have your friend play each one while you listen. Don't even look at the guitar while it's being played; just listen to what it sounds like. Because this is what you're going to sound like.

And make sure your friend (or the store salesperson if you're on your own) plays the sort of thing you'll be playing as a beginner—simple strummed chords for a start. If your friend plays something very fancy, you'll focus on the fancy playing and won't even notice the different sounds and tonal qualities each guitar has.

Also keep in mind that your new guitar is probably going to be only *part* of your purchase. You're going to want to get a case. Cases are often, but not always, included in the price of a guitar, so make certain before you buy your instrument whether or not a case comes with it.

Whether you play sitting or standing, it's good to have a guitar strap if you're going with an acoustic or electric guitar. And it certainly doesn't hurt to have picks (and extra picks) as well as a spare set of strings when you're just starting out.

If you buy an electric guitar, you're going to need an amplifier. Electric guitars (and acoustic-electric guitars) also need a cable (often called a "cord" or a "lead") to connect the guitar to the amplifier.

A tuner is essential and will last you a lifetime if you treat it well, although you will need to replace the batteries from time to time. And a guitar stand is certainly worth thinking about adding to the list, as are both a music stand and a metronome. If you've decided on a classical guitar, check out a footstool so you can play even more comfortably.

Most people play guitar right-handed—even many lefties, such as Paul Simon, David Byrne, and Mark Knopfler. If you're left-handed and undecided on which way to play, give yourself a simple test: without thinking about it, pick up a broom or a yardstick and pretend to play. Even playing "air guitar" will work. Take note of which hand is doing the strumming. Chances are likely it will be your left, and if so you'll want to seriously consider getting a left-handed guitar. Rhythm is essential to playing, and most guitarists prefer to leave that important job to their dominant hand.

If you buy your guitar at a store, be sure to have it *set-up* before it leaves the shop. A set-up for a guitar is a bit like a tune-up for a car. The guitar tech will check your instrument's action and intonation, as well as make sure there are no fretting problems. Often you'll get a cleaning and a fresh set of strings as well (although they may ask you to pay for the strings). Ask if your store includes a set-up as part of the cost when buying a new instrument, as many do.

Assess if you play left-handed or right-handed by noting which hand instinctively strums the guitar.

Classical Guitars

Classical guitars are the grand patriarch of the guitar family, direct descendants of the first six-string guitars that began to appear at the very end of the 1700s. Generally, they are slightly smaller than typical acoustic guitars (particularly the dreadnought style) but have a wider fingerboard, allowing for easy spacing of fingers on the frets, and slightly shorter necks (the fingerboard joins the body at the twelfth fret instead of the fourteenth, as most acoustics do).

Guitar Anatomy

Any guitar—classical, acoustic, or electric—can be broken down into three main parts: the headstock, the neck, and the body. All three types of guitars share many of the same parts, but each has its noticeable differences as well.

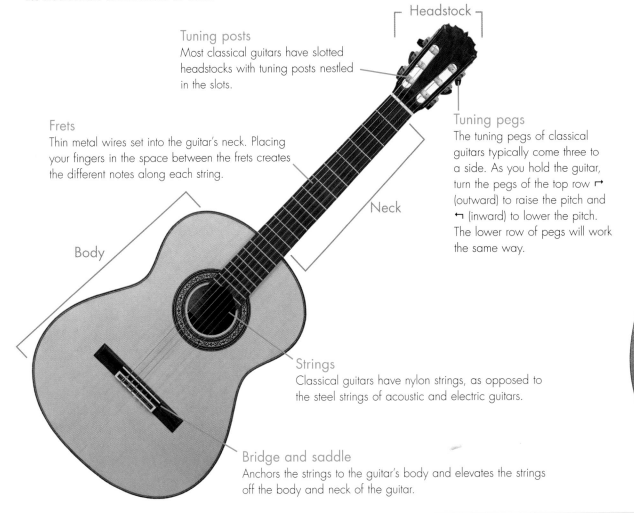

Headstock

Tuning posts
Most classical guitars have slotted headstocks with tuning posts nestled in the slots.

Frets
Thin metal wires set into the guitar's neck. Placing your fingers in the space between the frets creates the different notes along each string.

Tuning pegs
The tuning pegs of classical guitars typically come three to a side. As you hold the guitar, turn the pegs of the top row ↱ (outward) to raise the pitch and ↰ (inward) to lower the pitch. The lower row of pegs will work the same way.

Neck

Body

Strings
Classical guitars have nylon strings, as opposed to the steel strings of acoustic and electric guitars.

Bridge and saddle
Anchors the strings to the guitar's body and elevates the strings off the body and neck of the guitar.

Guitar Woods

Most guitarists prefer their classical and acoustic guitars to have "solid wood" tops, as opposed to wood laminates. Traditionally, the tops of most acoustic guitars are spruce, although the specific types of spruce can vary. Cedar is also used for the tops of guitar bodies, particularly on classical guitars and acoustic guitars marketed to fingerpicking players. But cedar is softer than spruce and scratches very easily.

Rosewood, mahogany, cherry, and maple are often used for the back and sides of a guitar, while rosewood and ebony are popular choices for the fretboard.

Flamenco Guitars

They may look almost exactly like classical guitars, but flamenco guitars are built with lighter, thinner tops to give the instrument's sound a bright percussive edge and more volume than the typical classical guitar. The string action (the height of the strings from the frets) is also set lower than that of a classical guitar.

Many guitar manufacturers also produce "half-sized" and "three-quarters sized" guitars, which are often referred to as "student guitars." Not that long ago you could only find student guitars in the classical style, but nowadays they come in acoustic and electric models as well.

Ramirez 1880 flamenco guitar.

Acoustic Guitars

Any non-amplified guitar is technically an "acoustic" guitar, but nowadays the term "acoustic" applies mainly to flat-top steel-string guitars, as opposed to classical guitars or arch-top guitars. Of the three main types of guitars, acoustics are the most widely played. They are great for both strumming (with or without a pick) and fingerstyle playing.

Guitar Anatomy

Depending on its body style, the acoustic is usually slightly larger than the classical and the neck is slightly narrower. The acoustic is usually also louder, considerably so when strummed with a pick.

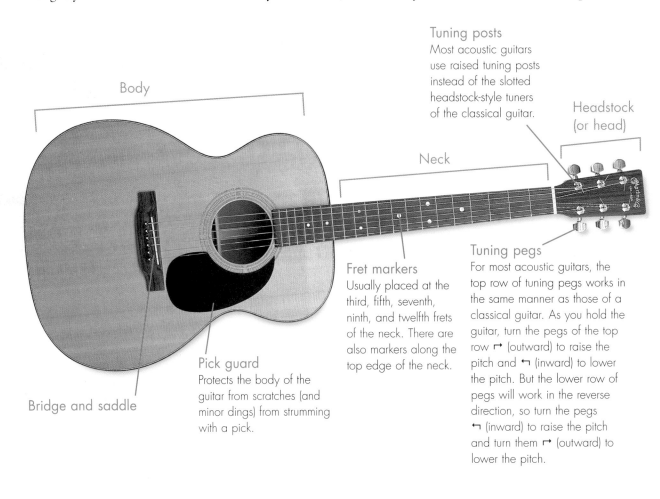

Body

Tuning posts
Most acoustic guitars use raised tuning posts instead of the slotted headstock-style tuners of the classical guitar.

Headstock (or head)

Neck

Fret markers
Usually placed at the third, fifth, seventh, ninth, and twelfth frets of the neck. There are also markers along the top edge of the neck.

Tuning pegs
For most acoustic guitars, the top row of tuning pegs works in the same manner as those of a classical guitar. As you hold the guitar, turn the pegs of the top row ↱ (outward) to raise the pitch and ↰ (inward) to lower the pitch. But the lower row of pegs will work in the reverse direction, so turn the pegs ↰ (inward) to raise the pitch and turn them ↱ (outward) to lower the pitch.

Pick guard
Protects the body of the guitar from scratches (and minor dings) from strumming with a pick.

Bridge and saddle

Acoustic Guitar Body Shapes

Acoustic guitars usually come in one of three primary body shapes: the dreadnought, the folk (also called concert, parlor, or auditorium), and the jumbo.

Dreadnought

Most acoustic guitars are dreadnought style. They are boomy and bassy and great for strumming. Compared to other styles, the dreadnought is boxier, with fewer curves to the shoulders and hips. It's usually also slightly larger in depth, and these two factors can make dreadnoughts uncomfortable to play for those with short arms.

Folk/Concert/Parlor/Auditorium

Folk-style guitars are almost identical to classical guitars in terms of size and shape, but still have a slightly thinner neck than the classical. Many guitarists find them perfectly suited to fingerstyle playing, as they have a good balance between the bass notes and treble notes.

Jumbo

Jumbos give you the best of both worlds. Their folk-style shape combined with the larger size and dreadnought-style depth give you both clarity and deep, rich tones.

Other Acoustic Guitar Types

Since the very first guitars, people have been modifying and adapting them in different ways. Here are three you may be interested in at some point further down the road in your guitar adventures.

- **Acoustic-electric** guitars are fitted with transducers or microphones (or both) that pick up the sound and send the signal via a cable to an amplifier or sound system.

- **Twelve-string** guitars produce an incredibly full and complex sound, because each string is paired with an additional close-set string that's tuned one octave higher for the four low strings and at the same pitch for the two high strings. Fretted and picked at the same time, the basics of playing is no different on a twelve-string than on a regular guitar.

- **Resonator** guitars are wooden- or metal-bodied and fitted with metallic cones inside that vibrate as you play to augment both volume and a twangy sound. You'll hear resonators in many types of music, but especially in blues, old-time music, and bluegrass.

Electric Guitars

When you think of rock 'n' roll, you think of electric guitars. Typically, electric guitars have thinner necks and lower string action than either the classical or acoustic, making them somewhat easier for people to play. But the thinner necks can be a challenge to making chords if you have big fingers.

Guitar Anatomy

Despite their many different varieties of shapes and sizes, electric guitars share many of the same standard features as classical and acoustic guitars. But they also have some specific characteristics all their own. Here is a basic rundown of the various parts of a typical electric guitar.

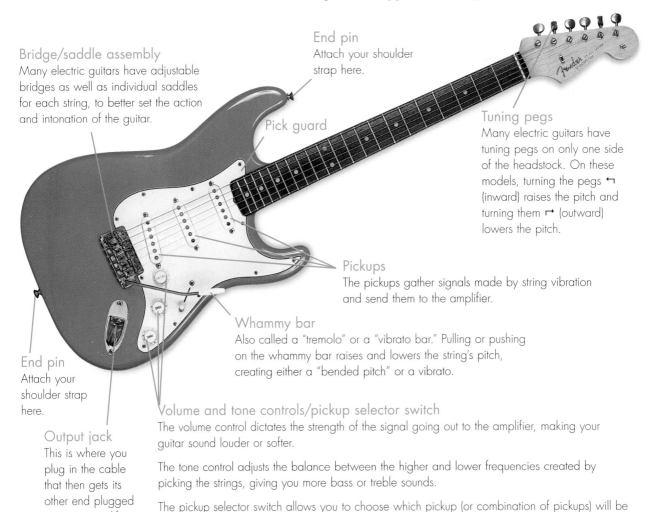

Bridge/saddle assembly
Many electric guitars have adjustable bridges as well as individual saddles for each string, to better set the action and intonation of the guitar.

End pin
Attach your shoulder strap here.

Pick guard

Tuning pegs
Many electric guitars have tuning pegs on only one side of the headstock. On these models, turning the pegs ↰ (inward) raises the pitch and turning them ↱ (outward) lowers the pitch.

Pickups
The pickups gather signals made by string vibration and send them to the amplifier.

Whammy bar
Also called a "tremolo" or a "vibrato bar." Pulling or pushing on the whammy bar raises and lowers the string's pitch, creating either a "bended pitch" or a vibrato.

End pin
Attach your shoulder strap here.

Output jack
This is where you plug in the cable that then gets its other end plugged into your amplifier.

Volume and tone controls/pickup selector switch
The volume control dictates the strength of the signal going out to the amplifier, making your guitar sound louder or softer.

The tone control adjusts the balance between the higher and lower frequencies created by picking the strings, giving you more bass or treble sounds.

The pickup selector switch allows you to choose which pickup (or combination of pickups) will be sending the signal to the amplifier.

Electric Guitar Body Styles

Electric guitars come in three basic body styles: solid, semi-hollow, and hollow.

Solid Body

The solid body is the most common, and its great sustain and loud amplification make it perfect for playing rock 'n' roll.

Hollow Body

The hollow body guitar is a favorite of jazz players. The fretboard is usually slightly wider, closer to that of an acoustic guitar. Jazz players will often fit their guitars with flat-wound strings to lessen unwanted string noise and overtones.

Semi-Hollow Body

Semi-hollow bodies are chambered, with a solid piece of wood running through the middle of the body. Both the hollow and semi-hollow guitars have a more acoustic sound, but amplifying them to higher volume levels will create feedback.

Electric Guitar Body Shapes

While electric guitars can come in almost any conceivable shape, most will be in one of three: the "Les Paul," "SG," or "Stratocaster/Telecaster" shape. Most other guitars are usually described in terms of their similarities to and differences from these models.

Les Paul

Usually the heaviest of these three shapes, it also produces heavy, fat tones with lots of sustain. They are ideal for both heavy rock rhythm playing and full-sounding lead lines.

SG

Like the Les Paul, the SG is heavy and great for rock 'n' roll. Also like the LP, it has a short-scale length (the distance from the bridge to the nut), which allows for easier bending and vibrato techniques.

Stratocaster/Telecaster

Stratocasters and telecasters pack a biting punch. Teles are especially twangy, while Strats can be both super clean and full of blues.

Changing Strings on Classical and Acoustic Guitars

Regardless of what type of guitar you have, changing strings involves two main steps—removing the old strings and putting on new ones. To remove the old strings, loosen each string to where it has a fair amount of slack, and then use a pair of wire cutters to cut the string between the nut and the tuning mechanism. Carefully remove the longer piece of string from the body of the guitar. Don't just pull the string through the bottom in a hurry—you might cause the string to scratch the finish of the guitar.

After you've removed the old string, you want to thread the new string onto the guitar down at the body. This process can involve different steps and methods, depending on the type of guitar you have.

Classical

On most classical guitars, you have to tie the strings onto the saddles, as shown here:

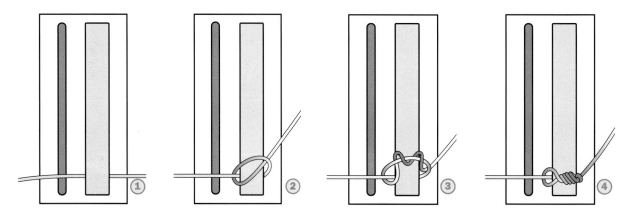

First, slip the string into the appropriate hole in the bridge and pull about 2 inches (5cm) out through the bottom of the bridge. Loop it around the string back at the top of the bridge and then braid the loose end around the portion of the string sitting on top of the bridge. Be sure to hold the longer section of the string (the side that's going up the neck) tight as you do so. You don't have to wrap it around the capstan, which is in the slots of the headstock, a lot of times. Most guitarists use only one braid on the capstan of the low strings and two or three on the high E and B strings.

Now wrap the other end of the string once around the appropriate tuning capstan. After wrapping it around once, push the end of the string through the hole in the tuning capstan so that you're trapping the string under itself. You're now ready to wind it to tighten the string to the correct note.

Acoustic

On most acoustic guitars, your strings will have a ball or circle of metal on one end. You want to put a kink in the ball end of the string, about an 1 inch (2.5cm) or so from the end.

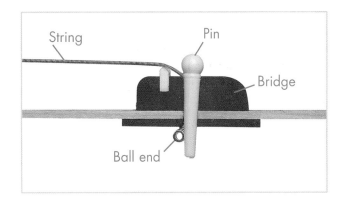

Next, thread the ball end of the string into the appropriate hole in the bridge and slip the string pin back into place. You don't have to (and you don't want to) press it in very hard.

Pull the loose end of the string somewhat taut, making certain the ball end stays snug in the bridge. Don't pull it so tight that you pull up the pin, which shouldn't happen if you've kinked the string as mentioned earlier! If necessary, hold one finger lightly on the string pin to hold it in place. Pass the rest of the string through the appropriate slot in the nut and thread it through the post hole of the appropriate tuner.

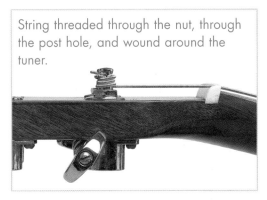

String threaded through the nut, through the post hole, and wound around the tuner.

After pulling the string taut, give it enough slack so that the string will be able to wrap about five times around the tuner. That's about 2 inches (5cm) for the wound strings and 3½ inches (9cm) for the unwound strings.

When you've given the string just enough slack, make a kink in the string on the far side of the tuning post (the side it came out of when you put it through the post hole) in the direction opposite of the way you're going to wind the tuner.

Start turning the tuner in the proper direction while, with your free hand, holding on to the string to keep even tension while the string wraps around the tuner. Make sure the string is still in its proper slot in the nut while you do this.

Obviously, if a single string breaks, you need to replace only that one, but what about if you want to replace all six? Guitarists constantly argue about whether it's best to change strings one at a time or to change all six at once. The main debate concerns whether removing all the strings at the same time changes the tension in the neck enough to damage it. The major advantage to changing all six strings at once is that you can give your fingerboard a thorough cleaning.

Changing Strings on Electric Guitars

On electric guitars, you usually find the holes for your strings either at the bridge or on the tailpiece of your guitar. Some guitars are "string through," meaning the hole through which you thread the string is in the *back* of the guitar.

If you have a locking bridge/nut system, you usually have to snip the ball off your string to fit it into the locking bridge mechanism. You can also buy strings without ball ends that are made especially for this type of tuning system. When you have the string in place on the bridge, you need to clamp the bridge, using an Allen wrench or other appropriate tool, before proceeding.

As you wind the string, you have to eventually (quite quickly, in fact) let go of it. Pluck it from time to time as you tighten it and check it against your electronic guitar tuner to see if it's in tune. You still want to stretch the string a bit, so tune the string slightly higher than the target note. For instance, if you're tuning the G string, tune it so it's maybe halfway between G and G♯. This will help stretch the string, but it's only the first step.

When you have the string tuned to a slightly higher pitch than normal, gently but firmly pull on the string with your fingers, directly up from the fretboard, as if you were drawing an arrow on a bow. Check the tuning again. You should have gone lower than the string's normal note. Retune the string, this time tuning it to the proper standard pitch. Repeat the "bow and arrow" pull, check the tuning again, and retune.

Stretching out the string and then tightening it keeps it from slipping once you get it in tune. Usually three "bow and arrow" pulls does the trick.

If you have a locking bridge/nut system, you've still got one more step. After you've replaced all the strings you plan to change, use the headstock tuners to get the strings tuned in normal fashion. Then set and lock the nut and use the microtuners to finish tuning all the strings.

General Maintenance and Care

Anytime you change all the strings of your guitar, you might also want to give it a thorough cleaning of the neck and frets. After removing all the strings, give the fingerboard a good going-over with a clean, dry cloth. A little fingerboard polish or oil (which you can get at most music stores) applied in small doses to the cloth—*not* directly onto the fingerboard—can help to keep it from drying out.

Whenever you play your guitar, it's good to take the time when you're finished to wipe the strings and even the body of the guitar with a clean, dry cloth.

You want to be smart about where you place your stand. Keep your guitar out of high-traffic areas, places where people and pets are constantly moving around and may accidentally knock into your guitar. Some people use wall hangers to prevent such mishaps.

And if you know you're not going to be playing for a much longer period of time than usual, put your guitar in its case and keep the case in a cool, dry location. Preferably keep it someplace inside your house, where it will get neither too hot nor too cold.

You also don't want to leave your guitar where it can get "overexposed" to the elements. Keep it away from heaters, radiators, air conditioners, and even constant direct sunlight whenever possible.

Remember that your guitar, just like you, wants to be comfortable. Not too hot, not too cool. Sometimes things are unavoidable—you may have to transport it in the trunk of your car, for instance. But keeping it in that hot trunk all day long is far worse than having it there for an hour or two.

Part 2

Warming Up to Play

Playing the guitar well means paying attention to little details. How you sit and hold your guitar, which part of your fingers you use to fret a note, and the motion you make when strumming all play a huge role.

In this section, you'll get a solid grasp of the basics to playing guitar, which, in turn, will make strumming, forming and changing chords, fingerpicking, and all the techniques you'll be learning as easy as possible.

The What and Where of Notes

Picking any one string of the guitar produces a note. Not just any note, but the note to which that string happens to be tuned. Pressing a finger onto the picked string at any place along the guitar's fretboard raises the pitch of the note.

Musical notes are given the names of the first seven letters of the alphabet, from A to G. And it's a given that these letters are cyclical; in other words, once you get to G the next letter will be A, and then it starts over again:

A   B   C   D   E   F   G   A   B   C   D   E...

These notes are written out on a musical staff—a set of five lines. You may remember the lines and spaces from school—the lines, from low to high, are E, G, B, D, F ("Every Good Boy Deserves Favor"), while the notes on the spaces—F, A, C, E—rhyme with "space."

At the far left of the staff is a treble *clef* (also called a G clef—the note G sits on the second line from the bottom of the staff, which is the line most crossed by the lines of the clef). Notes are added above and below the staff by use of *ledger lines*.

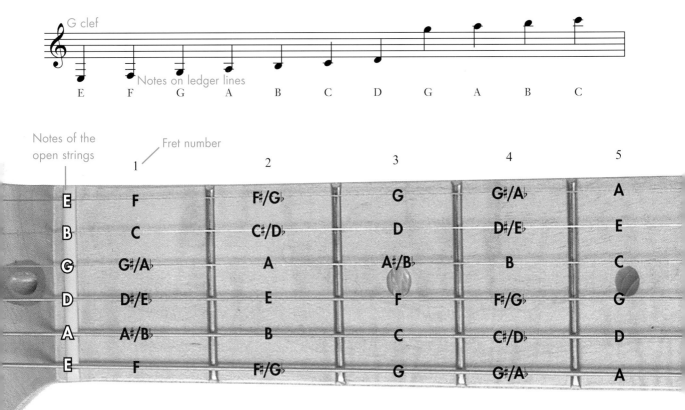

Additionally, there are notes called *accidentals*, which are marked by either *sharps* (♯) or *flats* (♭). "Sharp" is a musical half-step higher in tone, while "flat" is a musical half-step lower. This means that A♯ and B♭ are, technically, the same note, as are A♭ and G♯.

It's the "half-step" that is important to guitarists because each fret raises a note a half-step. Lining up all the notes on the D string, for instance, would look like this:

For now, though, concentrate on the non-accidental notes. Between the open strings and the third fret of your guitar, you'll find them here:

And in the chart at the bottom of these two pages, you'll find the notes for each of the first 12 frets of your guitar. Don't worry about memorizing them all at this point! But do take the time learn a few of them (especially the notes of the open strings!) and to understand their relationship to one another. Knowing that the third note of the A string is C, for instance, will help you out a lot when you start learning how to play the C chord.

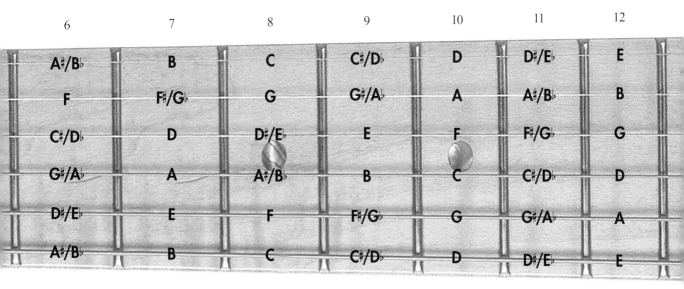

	6	7	8	9	10	11	12
	A♯/B♭	B	C	C♯/D♭	D	D♯/E♭	E
	F	F♯/G♭	G	G♯/A♭	A	A♯/B♭	B
	C♯/D♭	D	D♯/E♭	E	F	F♯/G♭	G
	G♯/A♭	A	A♯/B♭	B	C	C♯/D♭	D
	D♯/E♭	E	F	F♯/G♭	G	G♯/A♭	A
	A♯/B♭	B	C	C♯/D♭	D	D♯/E♭	E

Getting in Tune

Knowing the steps and half-steps between notes and where those notes are on the neck of your guitar will also help you to get your guitar in tune. In "standard tuning," your strings should be tuned to the notes shown.

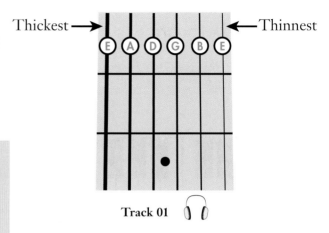

Thickest → E A D G B E ← Thinnest

Track 01

Know your string names! Some people use mnemonic phrases, like "**E**lephants **A**re **D**efinitely **G**oofy **B**efore **E**vening" to remember which notes each string is tuned to. Most people seem to like "**E**ddie **A**te **D**ynamite **G**ood **B**ye **E**ddie."

The easiest way to tune your guitar is with an electronic chromatic tuner. There are many types to choose from. Some have onboard microphones to hear and register the notes of your strings. Some you can plug your guitar directly into, assuming it's an electric or acoustic-electric guitar. Others clip onto your headstock, reading the vibrations of the string to determine its pitch.

With your tuner in place, strike the low E (the thickest) string. Your tuner's screen should indicate a note name (hopefully E!). Typically, you want the tuner's indicator to be pointing right at the center of the display. If the indicator is to the left, your note is flat; if the indicator is to the right, the note is sharp.

Obviously, if the note in the display is not E, you'll have to tune up or down to get into range. If you see C, C♯, D, or D♯, you're too low and need to tighten the string to raise it to the targeted pitch.

Adjusting tuning on a guitar.

Whenever possible, tune *up* to your target note. If your string is higher than it should be, loosen the string to lower than your target and then tune up to the target. Doing so keeps tension on the string and helps keep it in tune longer.

Tuning to a Keyboard or Piano

You can tune your guitar to a piano or keyboard. You'll need to know where middle C is on the piano, but once you do, you can easily find the notes of your strings.

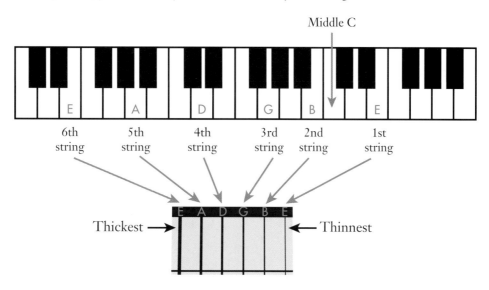

Relative Tuning

For those occasions you've no other method of tuning, use your newfound knowledge of the notes on the fretboard to tune to yourself.

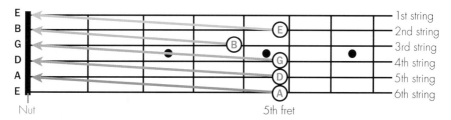

If you assume your low E string is in tune, you can then match the tone of the A note at the fifth fret to that of the open string and adjust it accordingly. The D note of the open D string is also at the fifth fret of the A string and the G note can be found at the fifth fret of the D string.

You match the open B string to the note at the fourth fret of the G string and then match the high E (first) string to the note at the fifth fret of the B string.

Holding the Guitar

How you hold your guitar can make all the difference in the world when it comes to playing clean and clear notes. Here are some tips:

Sitting

YES	NO

Sit straight with arms free and loose

Keep left hand at about chest level when fretting guitar

Guitar-side leg elevated

Guitar perpendicular to the floor and facing directly outward

Right arm holds guitar in place with gentle pressure

Curled posture tenses up arms and hands

Left wrist resting on leg makes it very hard to get optimal finger position on frets

Guitar tilted upward also makes fretting notes much more difficult

Right arm holds guitar too tight, making strumming very awkward

Standing

Stand straight with arms free and loose

Guitar neck angled upward (about two o'clock to someone facing you)

Keep left hand at about chest level when fretting guitar

Guitar body at good height to strum easily

Guitar perpendicular to floor and facing directly outward

Guitar strap feels comfortable and doesn't dig into shoulder

Weight balanced evenly between both feet

Hunched shoulders offer little ease of arm movement for either fretting or strumming

Neck angled too low makes fretting difficult (and can also lead to serious wrist injury)

Guitar body too low to strum effectively

Guitar turned upward decreases optimal finger placement on neck

Guitar strap not secure on shoulder, may slide off

Weight not balanced evenly between both feet

Classical guitar players typically place the guitar on their left leg, which is elevated slightly by a small footstool.

The Right Hand

Whether you strum your guitar strings with your fingers or with a pick, you have three basic choices: picking *across* the strings (in a motion parallel to the guitar's face), picking *into* the strings (pushing the string toward the face), and picking *away* from the face of the guitar.

As a beginner, you should focus on the first style. It will give you the best sound, while allowing you to develop both dexterity and speed with your picking and strumming—again, whether you use a pick or your fingers to strike the strings.

Basic Technique Using Your Thumb

Strumming down with the thumb, use the side or the corner of the tip of your thumb, keeping it parallel with the face of the guitar. Pushing in toward the face will get your thumb caught up in the strings, disrupting your rhythm. Pulling outward on the strings takes your thumb away from the other strings, making you lose time getting your thumb back in place.

Effective and efficient strumming, both with a pick and with your fingers, begins with your wrist and not your arm. Use a motion like turning a doorknob. The movement comes from your wrist and forearm; your elbow should barely move.

Strumming upward with a finger (or a few fingers), you want to catch just two to four strings. Striking all six strings on an upstroke will muddy the sound. Essentially, the purpose of the upstroke is to position your thumb and fingers for the next downstroke, so think of it as a cocking motion for the thumb.

You can strum in both directions while holding your thumb and fingers fairly close together, as if you were holding a guitar pick.

The Right Hand (continued)

Holding a Pick Properly

When you strum with a pick, you want to hold it in a relaxed but firm manner.

Leave just a little of the pick, only a quarter-inch or so, extending out from your fingers. Playing with too much pick often results in the pick getting caught on the guitar strings and falling out of your grip.

Position the pick against the string where you want to start your strum (it won't always be the low E string!), setting it perpendicular to the string.

Use a steady, even downward motion, keeping the pick as perpendicular to the strings as you can. Don't dig in toward the face of the guitar or flick the pick outward and away from the strings.

Picks come in all shapes, sizes, and thicknesses. As a beginner, you may be tempted to use thin picks, but they require more control when it comes to strumming and picking individual strings. Try out medium gauge picks to start and then experiment with others once you have a bit of confidence in your ability to use a pick.

The Upstroke

Once you've cleared the high E string, stop your strum. You'll have a lot more control over this if you're using your wrist and not your entire forearm for your strumming motion. Get into the habit of using short, measured downstrokes. The less motion you expend, the smoother your strumming will become.

On the upstroke, catch just a few strings in a short motion slightly *away* from the face of the guitar. Think of it as turning a key in a lock. This keeps you from strumming all the strings on the upstroke, which muddies the sound, and also sets you up nicely for the next downstroke.

There are many ways of strumming, and each will give your playing different tonal qualities. Using your nails on your strums produces a hard percussive edge, as does flicking out a finger or two in a downstroke. The flesh of your fingers provides a mellower tone, particularly on upstrokes.

The Left Hand

There are two essential steps to fretting notes cleanly on your guitar—knowing exactly what part of your finger to use on the neck and knowing that, as a beginner, you're likely to do a number of things that inadvertently keep you from optimally fretting with your left hand.

You want to use the very tips of your fingers to fret the strings. Hold your fingers up to your face as if you were going to poke yourself in the eye and you'll see exactly where your fingertips are.

You want to gently hold the guitar's neck *with* the left hand and not grasp it *in* your hand.

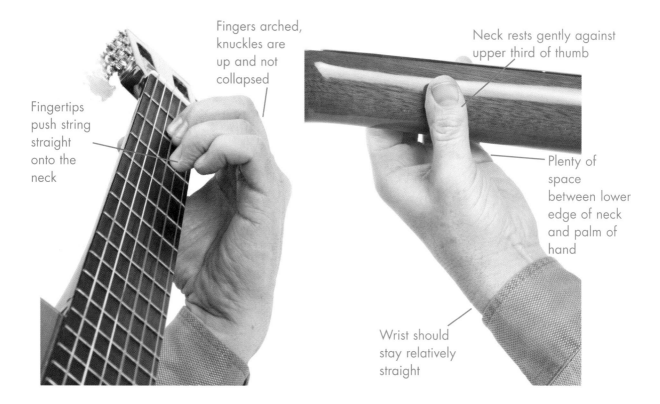

Fingertips push string straight onto the neck

Fingers arched, knuckles are up and not collapsed

Neck rests gently against upper third of thumb

Plenty of space between lower edge of neck and palm of hand

Wrist should stay relatively straight

Remember that your left hand isn't the one supporting the guitar and holding it in place. Try this demonstration: pick up a drinking glass or a plastic bottle of water and notice two things. First, your thumb most likely is placed directly opposite and almost exactly between your first two fingers. Second, you're not holding the glass or bottle like a baseball bat or a hockey stick.

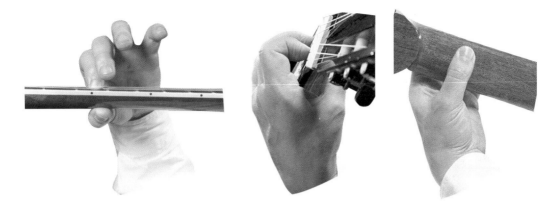

This may seem like an adequate finger position, but the lack of clearance along the lower edge of the neck (middle photo) will likely cause muting of the thinnest strings.

Let your thumb relax and follow the fingers as they move up and down the neck. Anchoring your thumb by grabbing the neck with it means your thumb is limiting finger movement, usually at the cost of fretting with the fingertips.

When fretting notes, your finger should be between the middle of the fret and the fret closer to the body of the guitar.

Keep all your fingers arched and close to the strings. When fretting, push the string directly onto the neck, taking care not to accidently push or pull the string to one side. You don't need as much pressure to fret the strings as you might think.

On top of all this, keep an eye both on your posture and on holding the guitar correctly. Sitting and standing straight with good posture will help you maintain a relaxed and comfortable position for your arms, wrists, and hands.

Holding the guitar will initially be a challenge simply because you're going to want to see your fingers on the fretboard and you'll tilt the guitar face upward so you can. Doing so, however, places your hands in a way that you can't fret the strings optimally with your fingertips. Too much tilt and your fingers will have little to no clearance on adjoining strings. This can't be helped at first, but when you know where your fingers should go, reposition your guitar so that the face is pointing directly outward and you should find your fingers having a much easier time fretting their notes.

Reading Guitar Tablature

You don't have to read music to play guitar (although it is helpful, and easier to do than you think!). But you're going to need some directions to follow. That's where guitar tablature (or "tab," for short) comes in.

In guitar tablature, you get a staff of six lines. Each line represents a string on your guitar. Numbers from 0 to 21 or 22 are placed on the lines of the staff. These indicate the fret you want to play on the designated string. You read tablature from right to left, regardless of what string a number may be on. Here's the first line of "Auld Lang Syne" to demonstrate:

Track 02

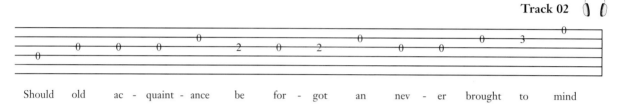

Should old ac - quaint - ance be for - got an nev - er brought to mind

To help you get acclimated to guitar tablature, start with some simple warm-up exercises, often called "one finger, one fret" exercises. Not only will you get some practice reading tabs, you'll also start working on using all your fingers to fret notes along the neck of the guitar.

Track 03

Place the tip of your index finger on the first fret of the high E string, slightly down-center from the headstock.

Place your middle finger on the second fret of the high E string.

Place your ring finger on the third fret of the high E string.

Place your pinky on the fourth fret of the high E string.

Here are a number of warm-up exercises for you. Concentrate first on simply getting good, clear, and clean-sounding notes. If any note sounds off or muted, recheck your finger's position on the fret or whether or not you're on the tip of your finger.

Be sure to use the fingers indicated in each exercise—the finger numbers will be under each corresponding note in the tablature staff.

Track 04

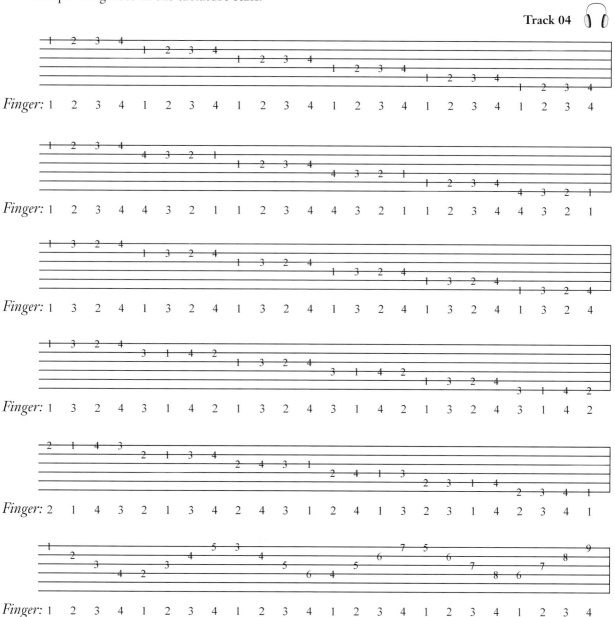

Reading Rhythm Notation

Guitar tablature only gives you part of the information you need. You also have to know just how long to play any note. For that, you'll need to know a little about standard music notation and rhythm notation.

Music is divided into *measures,* or "bars," each of which contains a set number of beats. At the beginning of a piece of music will be a *time signature,* usually consisting of two numbers stacked on one another. The top number (almost always 4 or 3) tells you how many beats each measure has while the bottom number (usually 4 for a quarter note or 8 for an eighth note) indicates which type of note is designated as "one beat."

Time signatures   *Measures*

Notes are given the following rhythmic values:

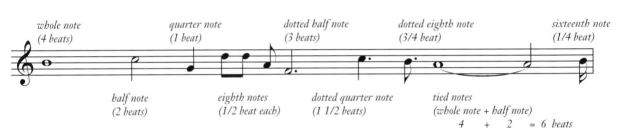

| *whole note* (4 beats) | | *quarter note* (1 beat) | | *dotted half note* (3 beats) | | *dotted eighth note* (3/4 beat) | | *sixteenth note* (1/4 beat) |

half note (2 beats)   *eighth notes* (1/2 beat each)   *dotted quarter note* (1 1/2 beats)   *tied notes* (whole note + half note)   4 + 2 = 6 beats

Be especially careful with the dotted notes (a dotted half note is 3 beats, a dotted quarter note is 1½ beats, and a dotted eighth note is ¾ of a beat) and the tied notes, which have the rhythmic value of the sum of the notes tied together. Take the time to learn and recognize these shapes. Most guitar music involves quarter notes, eighth notes, and sixteenth notes, as well as tied notes.

In *rhythm notation* you are only given a note's rhythm value and not its tonal value (indicated, as you've learned, by its placement on the staff). Here are the rhythm notation equivalents for the previous example:

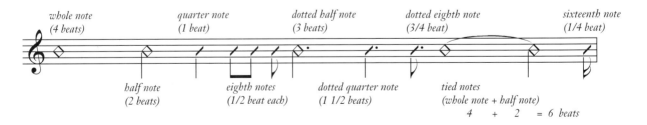

whole note (4 beats)   *quarter note* (1 beat)   *dotted half note* (3 beats)   *dotted eighth note* (3/4 beat)   *sixteenth note* (1/4 beat)

half note (2 beats)   *eighth notes* (1/2 beat each)   *dotted quarter note* (1 1/2 beats)   *tied notes* (whole note + half note)   4 + 2 = 6 beats

Here are some easy rhythm notation exercises for you to practice. To start out simply, these use only whole notes, half notes, quarter notes, and an occasional dotted half note. There are also a few tied notes, so be careful! Be sure to count slowly and evenly.

"Twinkle, Twinkle Little Star"

"Aura Lee"

"London Bridge"

Part 3

Getting Good with Rhythm

As a beginner, you want to focus first on learning chords and strumming in rhythm. Regardless of what styles of music you want to play—whether you want to be a classical guitarist, a singer/songwriter, or a heavy metal speed demon lead player—you have to be able to play in rhythm. And knowing your basic chords will prepare you for just about every intermediate and advanced technique you could ever want to learn.

In this section, you'll find how easy it is to keep a steady rhythm and to switch smoothly from one chord to another. You'll also pick up some cool tips on different styles of strumming and learn how to add simple bass lines as a part of your rhythm playing.

Your First Easy Chords

It's time to learn some chords to play so you can put all you've learned so far to good use! Chords are groups of three or more different notes played at the same time. First, you need to learn how to read chord charts and to use that knowledge to play chords on your guitar. Use E minor as your first step.

E minor

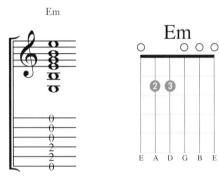

The Em (E minor) chord is one of the simplest basic chords to play. Finger 2 sits on the A string at the second fret and finger 3 is on the D string at the second fret as well. You can use whichever fingers you'd like, but using fingers 2 and 3 as indicated will prepare you for the upcoming E and Am chord changes.

E (E Major)

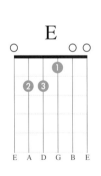

Keeping your Em chord in place, add finger 1 to the first fret of the G string. Play each string individually to make certain each note rings clean and clear. If the G string is not sounding clearly, make sure that finger 3 on the D string is on its tip and not brushing against and muting the G string.

A minor

Am

"X" indicates do not strike this string when you strum

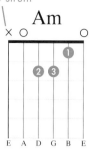

Now take your E chord and shift each finger one string closer to the floor. Finger 2 is now on the D string's second fret, finger 3 on the G string's the second fret, and finger 1 on the B string's first fret. When strumming, start your downstroke on the A string, skipping the low E string.

A (A Major)

A

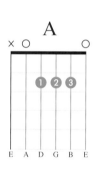

A (A Major) is the tricky chord of the first four. As shown in this illustration, you want to use finger 3 on the second fret of the B string, finger 2 on the second fret of the G string, and finger 1 on the second fret of the D string.

Many people find this fingering a little cramped! It's hard to get all three fingers side by side in one fret. If you have trouble with that fingering, try it instead with finger 2 up on the D string and finger 1 down on the G string. This fingering is helpful when switching to the E or D chords, which get played a lot with the A chord.

More Easy Chords

These seventh chords (which you'll learn more about soon) are some cool and easy twists on the chords you've just learned:

E7

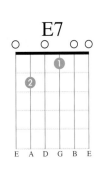

To play E7, start by playing an E chord. Then raise finger 3 off the D string. Play each string individually to make certain each note rings clean and clear. If the D or G string doesn't sound clear, make sure finger 2 on the A string is not inadvertently brushing against and muting the D or G string.

Em7

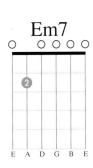

Em7, likewise, is an Em chord without finger 3 on the D string. It's the absolute easiest chord using all six strings that you'll ever play.

A7

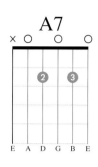

A7 is an A major chord with the G string open, so make your A chord from the previous page and just lift off whichever finger you have on the G string. Again, be sure the finger you have on the second fret of the D string stays on its tip and doesn't blunt the G string.

Am7

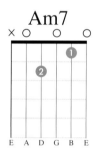

And you've probably already guessed that Am7 is your Am chord without finger 3 on the G string. This is a good chord to practice to prepare for the C chord, which you'll learn later.

You should always try out alternative fingerings for every chord you learn. You might find a variation that allows you to play a chord more comfortably and cleanly. Plus, chord charts never take into account which chord you played before and after the chord depicted in a chart. Changing from one chord to another can often be done more efficiently if you know alternative ways to play them.

More Easy Chords (continued)

Here are two more easy chords:

D (D Major)

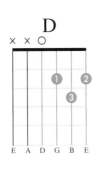

To make D, start with an A7 chord. But fret this particular A7 with finger 2 on the second fret of the B string and finger 1 on the second fret of the D string. Keep both fingers on the same frets but move them one string closer to the floor. Finger 1 is now on the second fret of the high E string while finger 2 is on the second fret of the G string. Try to line these two fingers over one another as much as possible. Then drop finger 3 onto the third fret of the B string. Be sure to keep all three fingers arched and on their tips to ensure clean, ringing notes.

D7

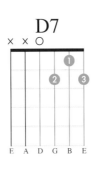

D7 is almost a mirror image of D, but it requires totally different fingering. Finger 3 is on the second fret of the high E string, finger 1 is on the first fret of the B string, and finger 2 is on the second fret of the G string.

These next two chords, while fairly easy, will get you to stretch your reach a bit. It's good to get started doing so early!

Dm

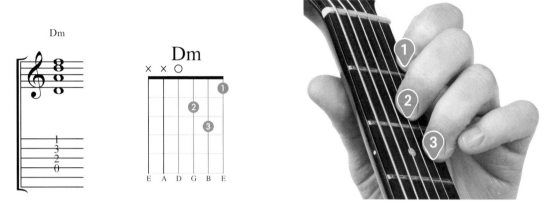

For Dm, use finger 1 on the first fret of the high E string, finger 3 on the third fret of the B string, and finger 2 on the second fret of the G string.

Some players find it more comfortable to use finger 4 (the pinky) in place of finger 3 on the third fret of the B string. Try it both ways and see which one is better for you.

Be sure to note the "×"s over *both* the low E string and the A string for all three of these chords. You want to start your strum for D, D7, and Dm on the D string, which means missing the two strings closest to you on the downstroke.

B7

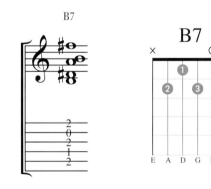

For the B7 chord, you'll need all four of your fingers. Start by playing an E chord. Keeping finger 2 in place, shift finger 1 to the D string's first fret and finger 3 to the G string's second fret. Finally, add finger 4 to the second fret of the high string. This is the first time you've used all four fingers on a single chord, so be patient and persistent as the B7 requires. Don't play the low E string.

Making Chord Changes in Rhythm

Learning how to play chords—recognizing the chord's name and knowing exactly on which frets to place your fingers—is the first of your two biggest steps as a beginning guitarist. The next one is to learn to change from one chord to another and to do so while keeping a steady, constant rhythm.

As with learning chords, it's best to start very simply. Begin by forming an Em chord and then strum it slowly eight times, only on the downstroke of your strum.

It may seem obvious, but take note of the fact that you're currently only striking the strings on a downstroke. When you're making the motion of the upstroke (in order to be set for your next downstroke), you're not striking the strings.

Your first chord change is to go from Em to A7. How you decide to make this change depends on how you're fingering the Em chord. If you're using fingers 2 and 3, as you learned previously, then you want to shift both fingers toward the floor while staying on the same fret. Finger 2 will move from the second fret of the A string to the second fret of the D string, while finger 3 moves from the second fret of the D string to the second fret of the B string, like this:

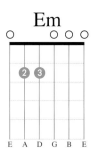

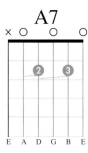

If you're fingering the Em chord with fingers 1 and 2, you can follow these same instructions, with finger 1 shifting from the A string to the D string and finger 2 from the D string to the B string.

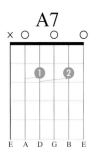

But you could also leave finger 2 in place on the second fret of the D string and drop finger 3 onto the second fret of the B string while lifting finger 1 off the A string, like this:

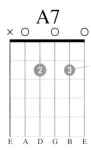

After practicing this chord change a few times, try it in rhythm, playing four beats of each chord:

Track 06

Set a slow pace and remember that you have the upstroke between the fourth and fifth beats to make your change. If you're not able to smoothly change between chords, slow down the tempo until you can. There's no such thing as too slow! Once you get comfortable making the change at whatever pace works, repetition of the chord change will build up muscle memory and you'll be picking up speed in no time.

Here are some more basic chord changes to try. Be sure to go through the same steps you just did with the Em to A7 change:

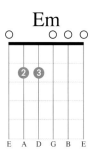
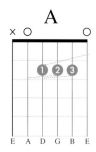
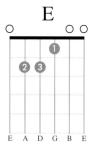
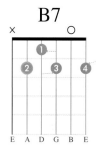

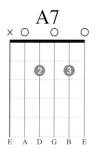
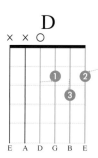
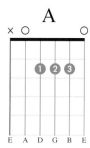
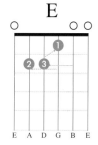

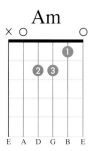
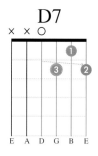
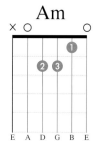
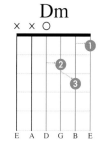

Making Chord Changes in Rhythm (continued)

When you've worked out as many combinations of two as you can, move up to combinations of three, like these:

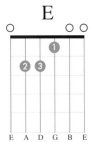

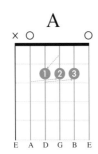

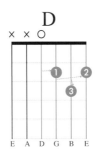

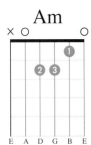

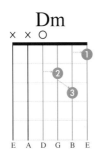

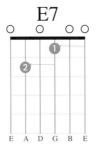

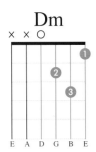

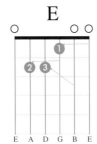

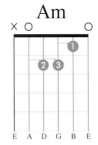

Each chord has a root note, the note that shares the same name as the chord. The root note of E, Em, or E7 is E. The root note of A, Am, or A7 is A. The root note of D, D7, or Dm is D. Remember that flats and sharps are part of note names, while majors, minors, and other numbers are part of chord names. You can know that the root note of Cm9 is C even if you have no idea how to play the chord! And the root note of F#13 is F#, not F.

Finally, try working on changing chords in combinations of four. Be sure to include returns to previous chords on occasion:

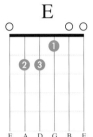

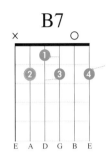

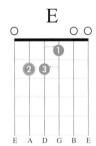

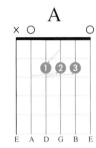

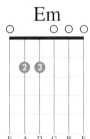

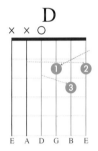

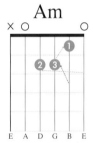

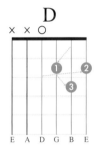

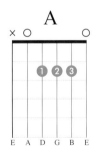

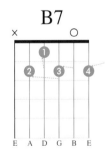

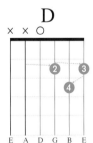

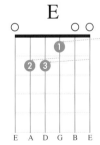

Root Notes and the "Bass/Strum"

Believe it or not, another way to practice making smooth chord changes is to not worry about getting the entire chord in place. At least, not at first!

Start by strumming eight Em chords again:

Now repeat those eight beats, but on the first beat of every measure, strike only the open low E string, which is the *root note* of the Em chord, like this:

Be sure to strike only the E string and only on the first beat of each measure. When you play the rest of the Em chord on beats 2, 3, and 4, start your strum on the A string.

This way of playing sounds a little more musical than just strumming the chord four times. It sounds even better when you hit the root note on the first and third beats of each measure, like this:

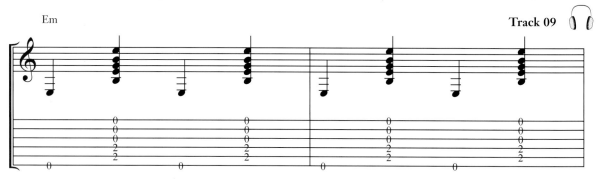

This style of playing goes by the name "bass/strum," for obvious reasons. You'll also hear it called the "boom-chuck" method.

Test the bass/strum on A. You'll hit the note of the open A string on the first and third beats and strum the rest of the A chord from the D string downward on the second and fourth beats:

Also try your new strum on the D chord:

Now go back and play your Em to A7 chord change using the bass/strum approach:

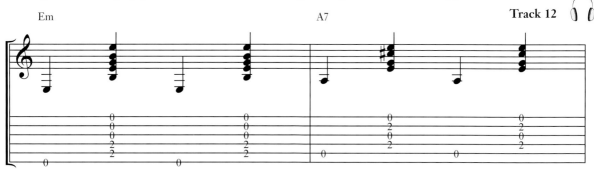

Hopefully you've noticed something very cool. Because you're hitting just the open A string on the first beat of the A7 chord change, you don't have to play the whole chord until the second beat. You've given yourself a bit of breathing room to help you make the chord change.

Practice: Root Notes and Bass/Strum

This "buying yourself time" during chord changes will only work with chords whose root notes are notes of open strings, but at this point it's a helpful tool. Plus, you're developing accuracy with your picking by practicing hitting single strings as well as strumming. All these skills will be very helpful in the future.

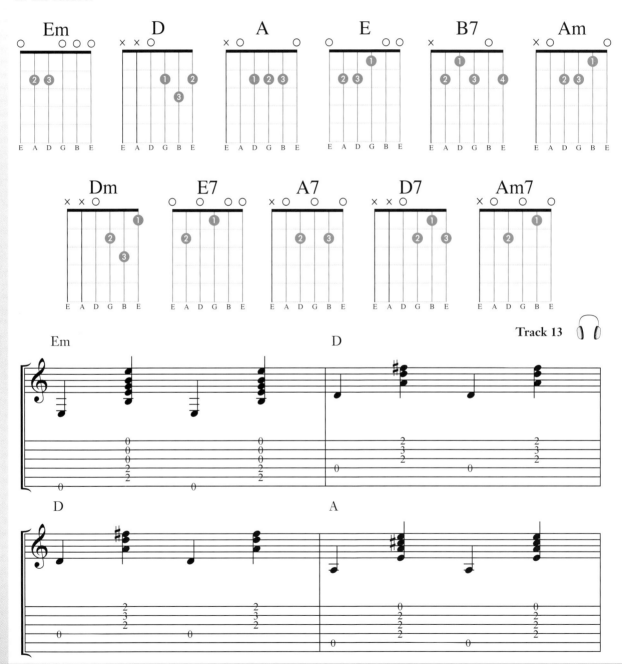

Alternating Bass

Learning the bass/strum technique also prepares you for playing in the alternating bass style, which will make your strumming sound even better.

In alternating bass playing, you will alternate your single bass notes between the chord's root note and another note of the chord being played. Don't worry! It's a lot simpler than it sounds.

Begin by playing an A7 chord in the bass/strum style:

This time through, play the open low E string on the third beat instead of the open A string. On the fourth beat, be sure to start the strum of the rest of the A7 chord on the D string, which means skipping both the low E and A strings:

The alternating bass sounds even more musical than the bass/strum! It's a style that's used in every genre of music.

> As soon as you feel comfortable playing an alternating bass pattern, try to play it without looking at your picking hand. It won't be pretty at first, but it will help you gain confidence in your picking abilities.

Now try playing the D chord in an alternating pattern, which will involve alternating between the open D and open A strings for your bass notes:

D

Track 16

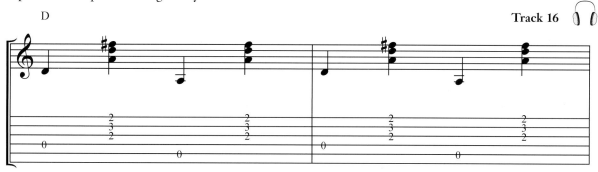

Playing alternating bass on E and Em chords is a little trickier. You're going to alternate between the E note of the open low E sting and the B note at the second fret of the A string, like this:

E

Track 17

Here you want to make your strums of the rest of the E chord from the D string on downward, so you have to skip the A string after hitting the low E string on the first beat. With a little practice, you'll be playing this pattern with relative ease.

And once you're at that level of comfort, try a little more challenging variation of the alternating bass pattern. For this pattern you want to start all your strums of the E chord from the G string downward. This will take some concentration, but again, with practice you'll surprise yourself at how quickly your fingers take to playing in this style.

E   A   Track 18

E chord with alternating bass over three strings   *A chord with alternating bass over three strings*

Practice: Alternating Bass with Chord Changes

These exercises combine the alternating bass patterns you've just learned with changing chords. Start simply with switching between two different chords per exercise:

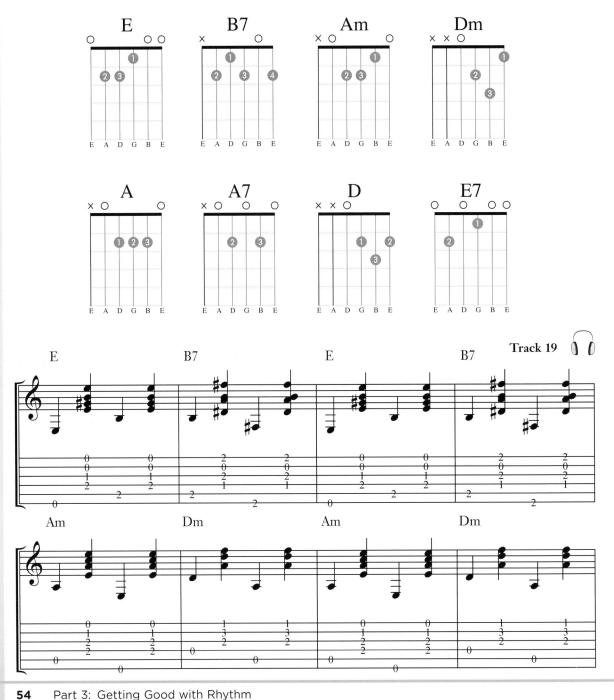

Now try working with three or four different chords in each exercise.

Practice: Alternating Bass Line

This arrangement of "Do Lord" is played with an alternating bass line throughout the whole song. You'll be using the A, A7, D, and E7 examples from the previous page.

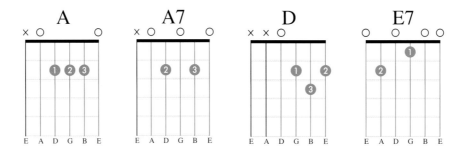

Track 20

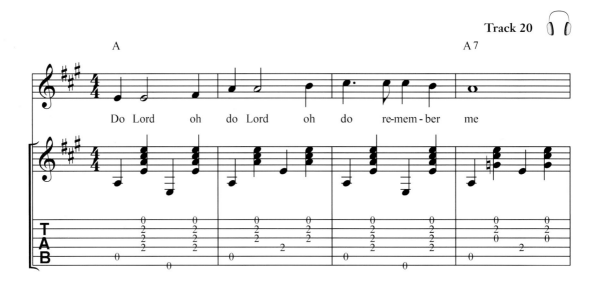

Strumming Eighth Notes

So far all of your strumming has been in steady, even downstrokes played in quarter notes. It's time to put your upstrokes to use, too.

> In music notation, tablature, and rhythm notation, downstrokes are usually indicated by marks that look like heavy-duty staples (⊓) and upstrokes are indicated by tall, thin V shapes (ᵛ).

As before, start with the Em chord, strummed on each beat with a downstroke:

Do this again, this time striking the strings on your upstroke as well. As you've learned, you want to catch just a few of the strings on your upstroke as you get your hand set for the next downstroke. Strumming all six strings on both the downstroke and upstroke will result in a very muddy sound.

Even if you're doing well catching only a few strings on the upstroke, playing constant down and up strokes with each beat can get tiring, to both your wrist and your ears. To make your strumming more musical, add an upstroke to just one beat per measure. Start with the first beat, like this:

Then move your upstroke to the second beat, then the third, and then the fourth:

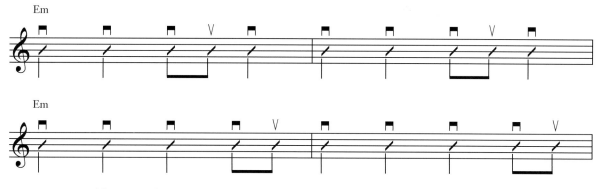

For variety, add a second upstroke per measure, and then a third:

Track 25

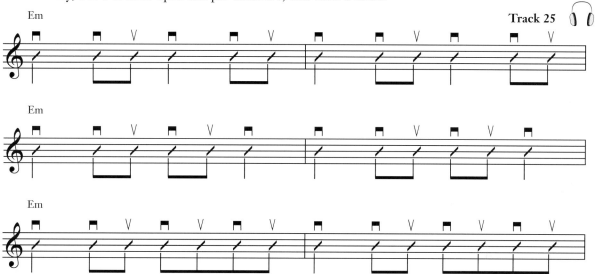

After you've gotten the hang of strumming in eighth notes, try adding in alternating bass patterns. Here are some exercises to get you started:

Track 26

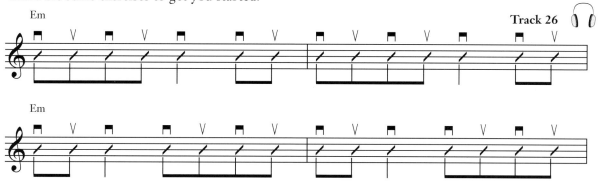

Practice: Eighth Note Strumming

Strumming in eighth notes is a large part of playing guitar, so it's important to practice keeping a steady beat and a consistent rhythm. The exercises on these two pages are here to help you do just that. First, you'll work on changing some of the patterns you've just learned from measure to measure.

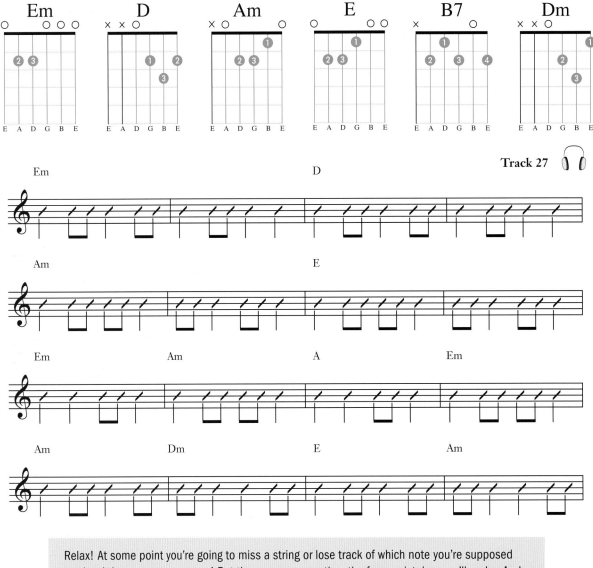

Relax! At some point you're going to miss a string or lose track of which note you're supposed to play. It happens to everyone! But the more you practice, the fewer mistakes you'll make. And you'll also find that you're becoming an accurate picker with a good feel for which string you're picking without having to look at it.

These eighth note strumming exercises involve changing chords and adding alternating bass patterns. Practice each one slowly at first until you can make each chord change at the proper time and in rhythm. Gradually pick up the tempo as you become more comfortable with each exercise.

Practice: Alternating Bass with Eighth Note Strum

You'll get a lot of practice with Em and Am chords in this arrangement of "Worried Man Blues," as well as a chance to practice both your alternating bass and the eighth note strums you've just picked up.

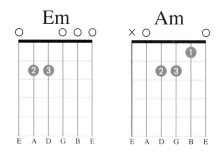

Track 29

Simple Syncopation

You've done a great job so far in learning rhythm and keeping a steady and even beat. The next step is to sound like you're off the beat even though you're still holding the overall rhythm steady and true.

Start by playing this simple rhythm. Be sure to listen to the count (or better yet, count along yourself!):

When you're comfortable, try missing the downstroke on the third beat. If you keep your strumming motion constant and even, you should find it fairly simple to do:

This sort of strum is called *syncopation*. The rhythm's accent has shifted from the beat to the offbeat (the "and" between the counts of the beat). It's an easy concept to grasp but most beginners need a fair amount of practice to get confident playing syncopated rhythms. Here are more exercises for you to practice:

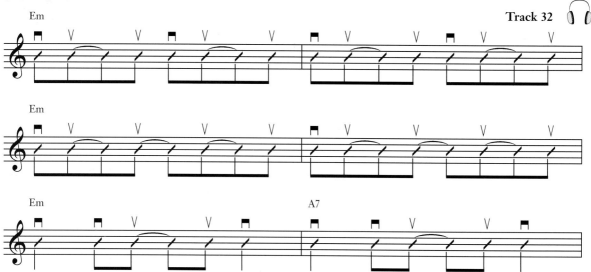

Introducing Suspended Chords

You can add a lot of spice to your syncopations with suspended chords. Basically, suspended chords (usually called "sus," "sus4," or "sus2") are slight variations of the regular chord. On the guitar, D, A, and E are excellent chords to use with suspended chords. Here are some examples:

Asus2

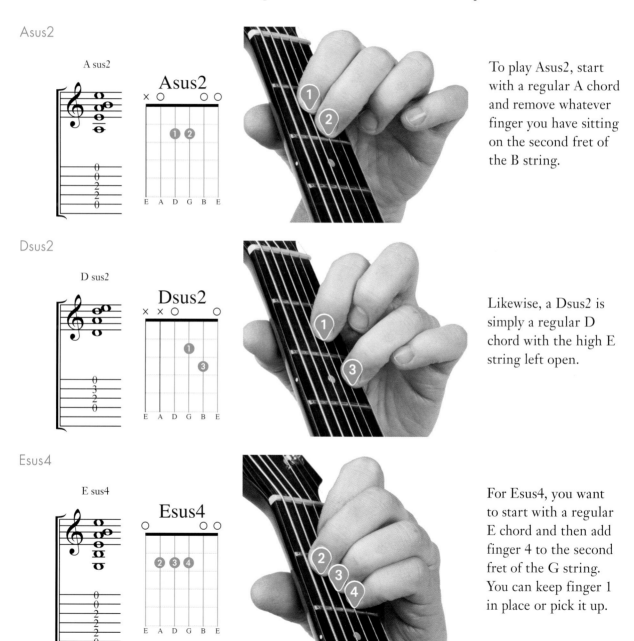

To play Asus2, start with a regular A chord and remove whatever finger you have sitting on the second fret of the B string.

Dsus2

Likewise, a Dsus2 is simply a regular D chord with the high E string left open.

Esus4

For Esus4, you want to start with a regular E chord and then add finger 4 to the second fret of the G string. You can keep finger 1 in place or pick it up.

Practice: Syncopation and Suspended Chords

Using a change to the suspended chord at the point of syncopation sounds very dramatic, but it will require you to become used to making a chord change on the upstroke. Use these examples to get some practice with syncopation and suspended chord techniques before taking on "My Bonnie Lies Over the Ocean."

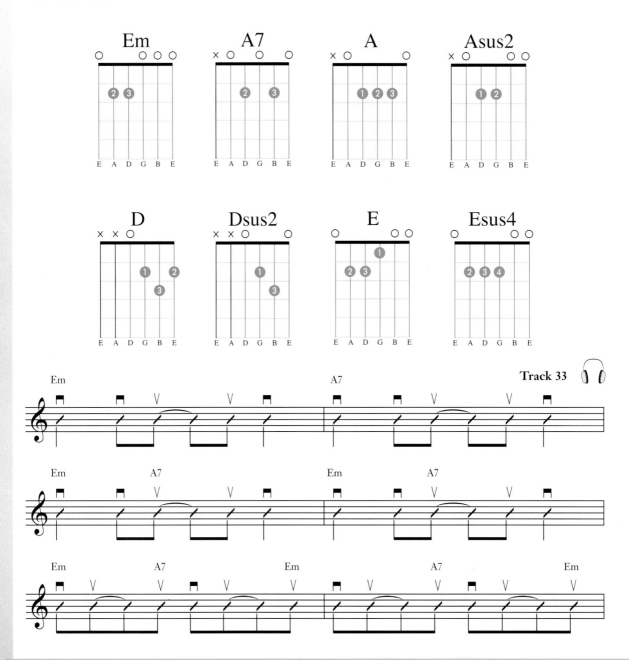

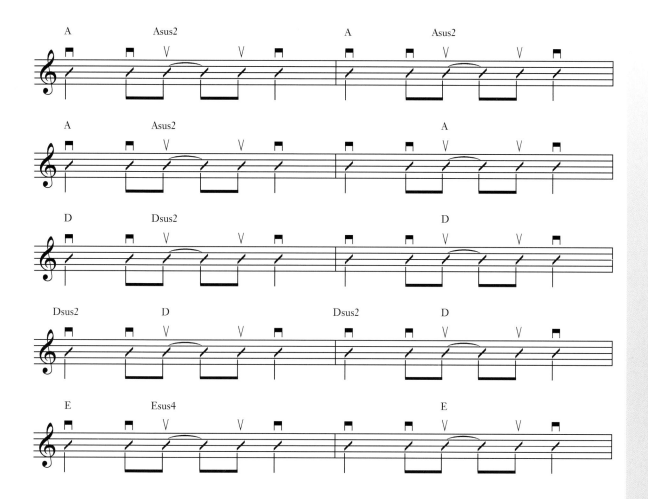

Practice: Syncopated Strumming

In this arrangement of "My Bonnie Lies Over the Ocean," all done with syncopated strums, you'll get more practice with the Asus2, Dsus2, and Esus4 chords.

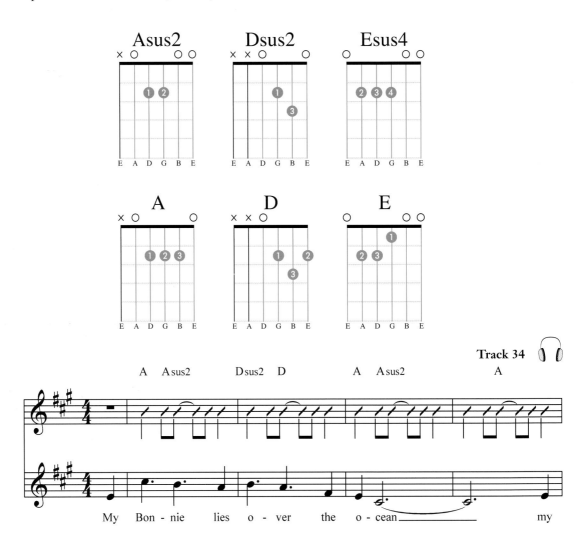

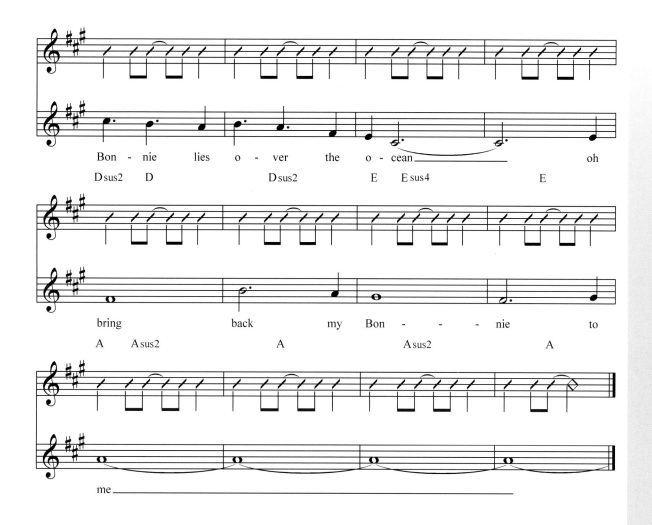

Bon - nie lies o - ver the o - cean_____ oh

D sus2   D   D sus2   E   E sus4   E

bring   back   my Bon - - nie   to

A A sus2   A   A sus2   A

me_____

Taking a Rest

Silence is as much a part of music as sound. Incorporating *rests*, or moments of silence, into your strumming is yet another way to create interesting rhythms.

Rests, like notes in standard and rhythmic notation, have specific shapes that denote their rhythmic value. You can have a whole rest (four beats), a half rest (two beats), a quarter rest (one beat), an eighth rest (a half beat), or a sixteenth rest (a quarter beat). You'll be reading about the corresponding sixteenth notes very shortly, but for now here are the symbols for each rest:

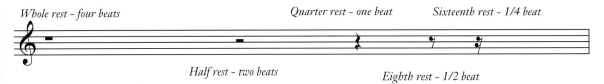

The most effective way of creating a rest is to lay your right hand gently on the strings to keep them from ringing. You can also lift the fingers of your left hand slightly off the strings after playing a chord, just enough to mute them.

Here are some very simple exercises to help you begin practicing making rests:

Track 35

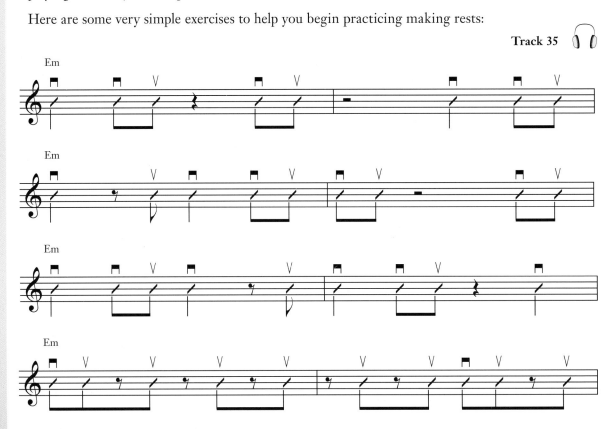

Combining Alternating Bass, Syncopation, and Rests

Here are a number of sample rhythms using combinations of quarter notes, eighth notes, alternating bass, syncopation, and rests. Take each one slowly and carefully until you can play it confidently. Then gradually increase the tempo of your strum.

Track 36

Practice: Rests, Alternating Bass, and Syncopation

"He's Got the Whole World in His Hands" uses just two chords, D and A7, so you can focus your attention on switching between alternating bass lines, syncopated strums, and the use of rests that you've been working on.

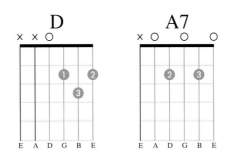

Track 37

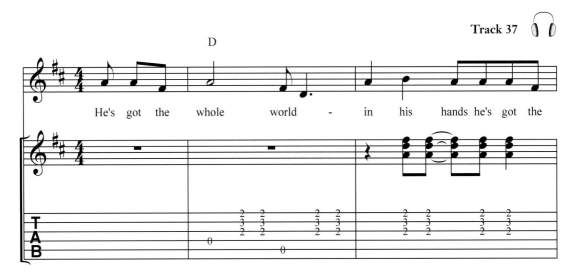

He's got the whole world - in his hands he's got the

Strumming Sixteenth Notes

Sixteenth notes have a rhythmic value of one quarter of a beat. That's pretty fast—so much so that trying to count out sixteenth notes is not easy. Here's how most musicians go about counting quarter notes, eighth notes, and sixteenth notes.

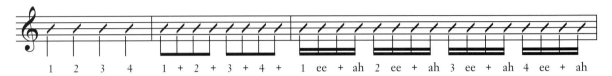

You want to get that "one ee and ah, two ee and ah, three ee and ah, four ee and ah" firmly in your head. Strumming sixteenth notes, you'll be making a downstroke on both the beat and the "and" between the beats. The upstrokes fall on the "ee" and the "ah" of each beat.

It's also important to know that while you're playing more notes, the tempo is still holding steady. Here's a great exercise to help you reinforce this idea:

Track 38

You can hear that the count is consistent throughout the exercise and that the eighth notes divide the beat evenly into two halves, while the sixteenth notes divide it evenly into fourths.

Let's try out a few basic sixteenth and quarter note rhythms to get you started:

Track 39

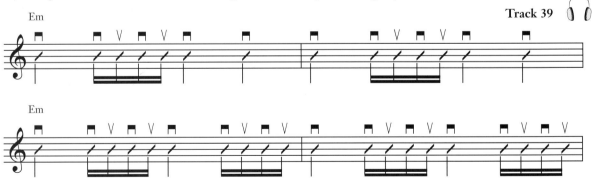

Here are a number of sample rhythms using a mix of quarter notes, eighth notes, and sixteenth notes for you to try out. Some involve only chords, some use alternating bass notes, and some even include a bit of syncopation. If you're the slightest bit unsure of how the rhythm should be played, count it out loud while you listen to help you get the beat firmly in your head and in your hands.

Practice: A Little Island Music

You can use sixteenth notes to give your rhythm playing more variety. And while it may seem like a small and subtle difference, changing your use of downstrokes and upstrokes can also greatly affect your sound. In some cases, you'll swear you're playing reggae!

Start with a basic bass strum, all in quarter notes:

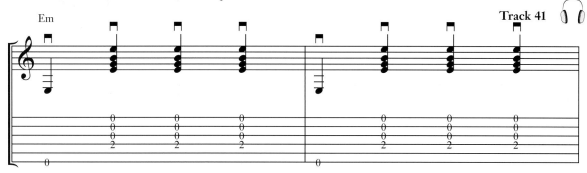

Now change the strum so that you're playing a bass note on each beat (as a downstroke) and the chord on the offbeat (with an upstroke):

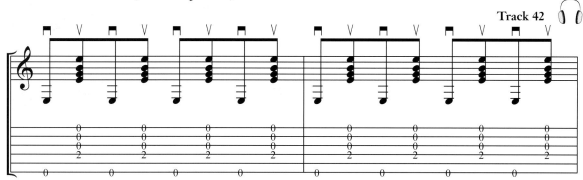

Finally, replace the eighth note of each chord with two sixteenth notes, playing both as upstrokes:

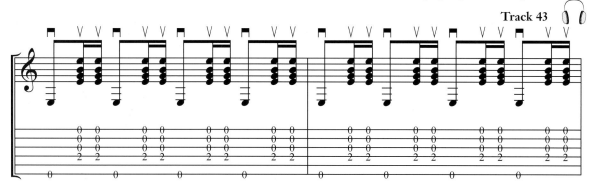

When you're comfortable with this, you can experiment by varying the pattern. Use a combination of eighth notes and sixteenth notes for the chords or use rests instead of the single bass notes. You can also try out alternating bass patterns:

Track 44

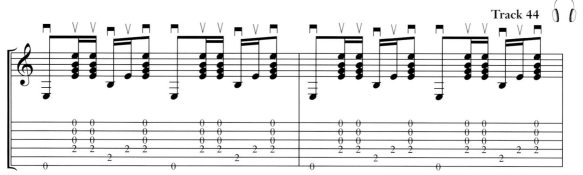

Pay close attention to the different alternating bass patterns used here in "Sinner Man." And don't be shy about experimenting and coming up with some of your own.

Track 45

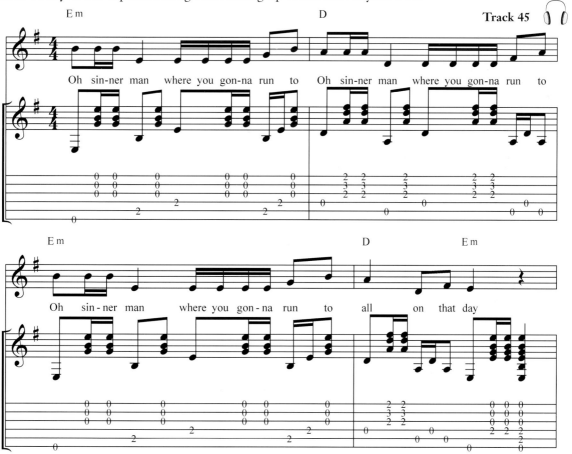

Triplets and Swing Rhythms

Just as eighth notes divide a single beat into half, triplets divide a single beat into even thirds. In both music notation and rhythmic notation, triplets look like eighth notes but are linked together with a small "3," like this:

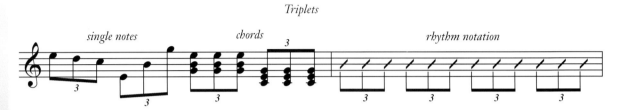

You can strum triplets with a regular "down and up" stroke, but most guitarists find it easier to start each beat with a downstroke, which requires developing a small hitch in your regular strumming:

Track 46

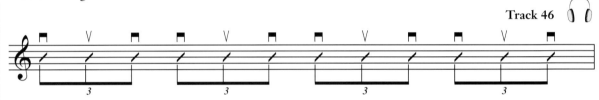

Both ways of strumming triplets work, so you have to practice each to determine which is most comfortable for you while keeping the rhythm steady and true.

Being comfortable playing triplets is important because triplets are the basis of *swing rhythm*. In swing, just the first and third of each triplet is played.

Track 47

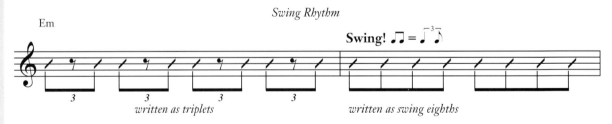

You can easily combine swing rhythms with an alternating bass by using quarter notes for the bass notes on the first and third beats and playing these "swing eighths" on the second and fourth beats. Be sure to note the little icon at the beginning of the example, which indicates that the piece is meant to be played in swing rhythm. To help you get the rhythm of this last example, count the beat as "one and ah two and ah three and ah four and ah," and strum only on the beat (the "one," "two," "three," and "four") as well as the "ahs."

This arrangement of "The Midnight Special" will help you practice strumming alternate bass patterns in a swing rhythm:

Double Stops and Shuffles

Being able to strike your strings accurately is important. You know from strumming A, Am, and D chords that you don't always want to hit all six strings. Sometimes you may want to strike just two. This is called a *double stop*. Practicing double stops will help you improve your picking accuracy and will also give you a step up with *shuffles*, which are an essential rhythm technique.

Here is an example of double stops to get you started:

Track 49

Double stops are commonly used to play shuffles. In a basic shuffle, you play a pair of notes—the low one usually being the root note of your chord and the high one being the fifth note in the scale of the root note (and you'll learn more about scales later). On the second and fourth beats of the shuffle, you will change the high note for the next note a full step higher (which is the sixth), like this:

Track 50

It already sounds like rock 'n' roll, doesn't it? Now on the third beat use the note a half-step higher (the flatted seventh) before going back to the sixth:

Track 51

You can also play these easy shuffles using either the open A string or the open D string as your root note:

Track 52

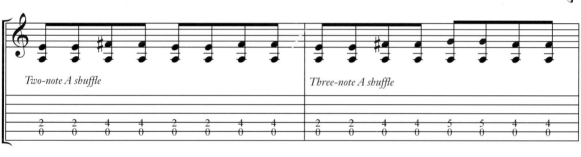

Double Stops and Shuffles (continued)

Now try the same shuffles but this time using swing rhythm:

Track 53

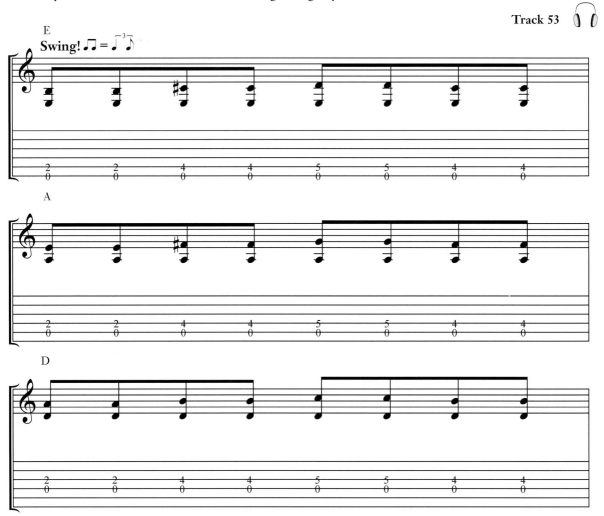

Shuffles played in swing rhythm are called "blues shuffles" or "swing shuffles," while shuffles played with regular eighth notes are often called "rock shuffles."

In "Frankie and Johnny," you'll be playing the B7 chord as an arpeggio, meaning you'll strum it one string at a time while holding on to the chord, like this:

Track 54

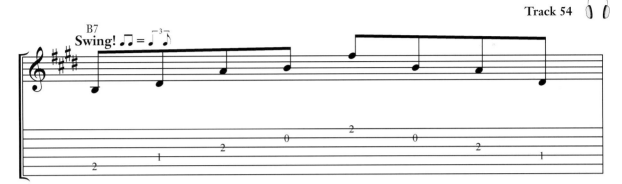

Remember that this will be in swing rhythm, so you want to keep that "one and ah two and ah three and ah four and ah" count going in your head as you play.

And, finally, here is a cool use of double stops that can be used to end a blues song:

Track 55

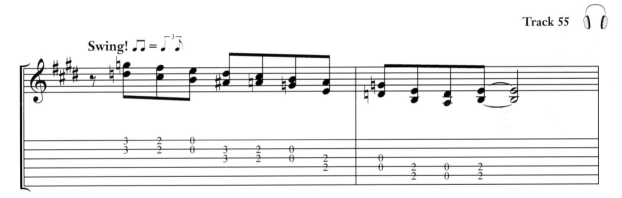

Practice: Shuffle Style

"Broke and Hungry" is played with a rock-shuffle style. It uses a combination of two-note and three-note shuffles, so pay close attention!

Track 56

The last line of "Frankie and Johnny," which is done in a blues shuffle, switches from a two-string shuffle to picking the single strings of a B7 chord. And watch out for the double stops in the next-to-last measure.

C and G Chords

G and C are two chords you're likely to use more than any of the ones you've learned to this point. They require more patience to learn than most of the other chords, too!

C

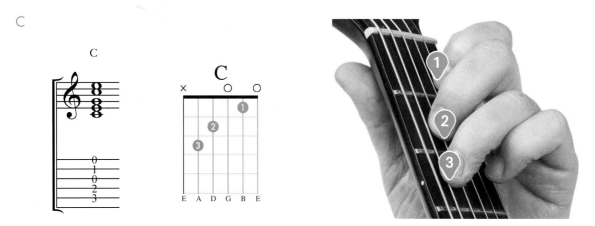

Start by forming an Am chord. Raise finger 3 off the D string, which gives you Am7. Now place finger 3 on the third fret of the A string. You may have to shift all your fingers a bit toward the body of the guitar. Make especially sure that all fingers are arched and not brushing against either the open G or the open high E string.

C7

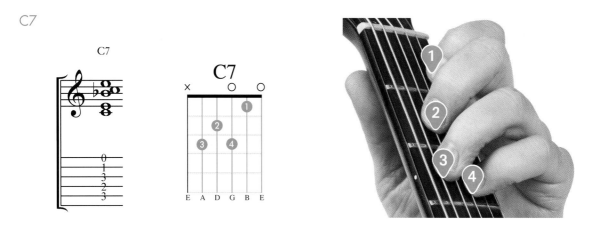

With your C chord in place, add finger 4 to the third fret of the G string.

G

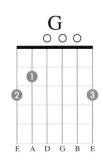

Place finger 2 on the third fret of the low E string. Then put finger 1 on the second fret of the A string and finish by placing finger 3 on the third fret of the high E string.

Some guitarists prefer to use the following fingering: finger 3 on the third fret of the low E string, finger 2 on the second fret of the A string, and finger 4 on the third fret of the high E string.

Here are two other possible ways to make a G chord:

G (1st variation)

For the 1st variation of G, start with the original G chord and use finger 4 on the third fret of the high E string and finger 3 on the third fret of the B string. This sounds slightly different than the "normal" G, so you want to make sure you want your G chord to sound that way.

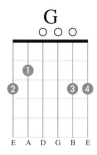

G (2nd variation)

The 2nd variation makes use of "string muting," which you'll learn more about later. Place finger 3 on the third fret of the high E string and finger 2 or finger 1 on the third fret of the low E string. Let the finger on the low E string brush against the open A string enough to muffle its sound, so when you strum through all six strings you won't notice the muted string but instead will hear the rest of the chord.

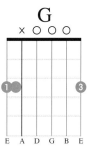

Practice: C and G Chord Changes

More often than not, you'll find C and G used with the D, Em, and Am chords. But, as always, you have to be ready to change to either C or G from any chord you know. Here are some sample progressions to try out.

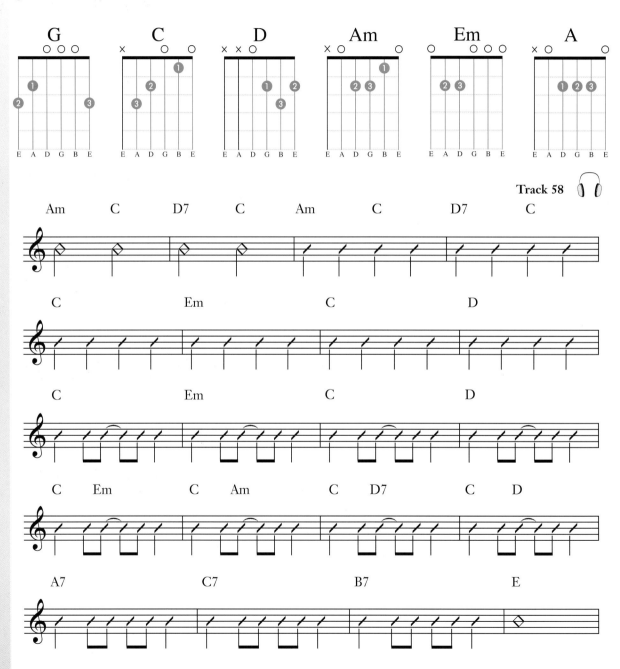

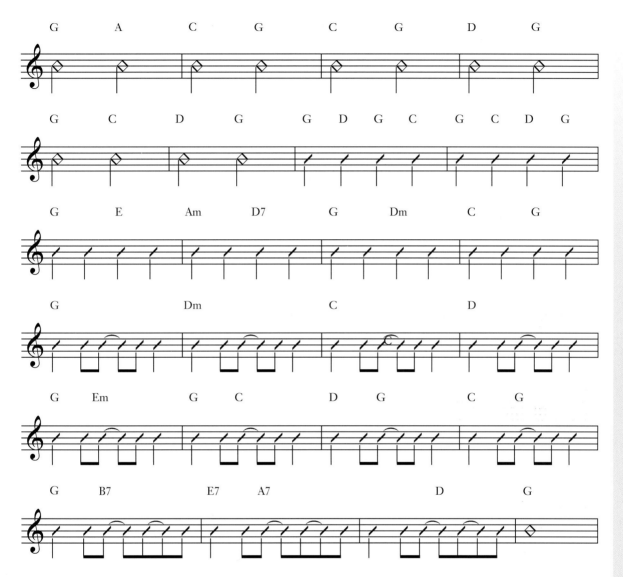

You also want to get in the habit of starting to form your C chord with finger 3. If you start out by placing finger 1 on the neck first, you'll find yourself waiting until all three fingers are in place to make your strum. Doing so will often create noticeable pauses in your rhythm.

Practice by focusing on the G to C switch. Hold the G in place and count to three and then try to get only finger 3 in its place as quickly and smoothly as possible. You'll notice that as you do, fingers 1 and 2 line up almost exactly where you want them to be to complete the C chord.

Walking Bass Lines

One way to get used to getting your fingers in place correctly for C and G chords is to incorporate walking bass lines into your strumming. A walking bass line is a bass line that moves from one note (usually the root note of the chord you're playing) to another (usually the root note of the next chord) by means of the notes between your two root notes.

Suppose you were alternating two measures of G with two measures of Em, like this:

You can add a simple walking bass line by playing just the G note (third fret of the low E string) on the third beat of the second measure and then the F♯ note (second fret of the low E string—use finger 1 to do so) on the fourth beat, like this:

Track 59

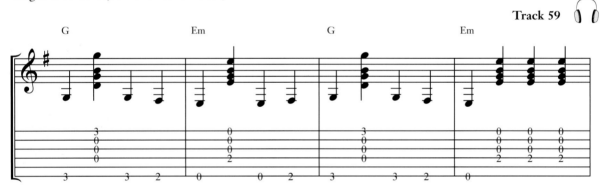

You can also reverse direction by playing the chords in reverse order. Going from C to Am and back to C would look like this:

Track 60

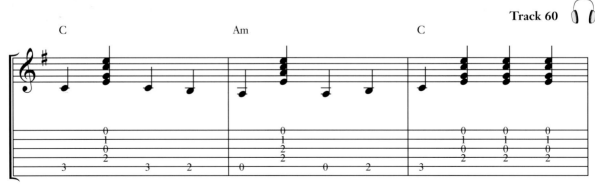

Moving from G to C is slightly more involved. After playing the G chord for five beats, strike just the G note in the bass. Then raise all your fingers (but not too far!) in order to both strike the open A string and readjust your position so you fret the following B note (second fret of the A string) with finger 2. This puts you in perfect position to use finger 3 on the C note (third fret of the A string), which kicks off the C chord.

Track 61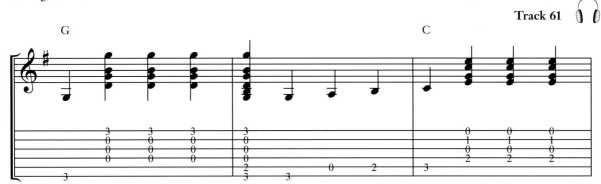

You can use the same idea to walk from G to D by moving directly from the B note (second fret of the A string) to the note of the open D string:

Track 62

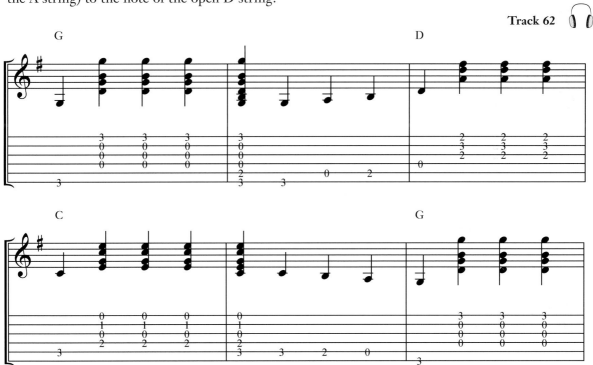

Practice: Walking Bass Lines

"Come and Go With Me" has walking bass lines from G to C, G to Em, and G to D, not to mention going back to G from C, Em, and D. You'll be doing a lot of work with your left hand on this song.

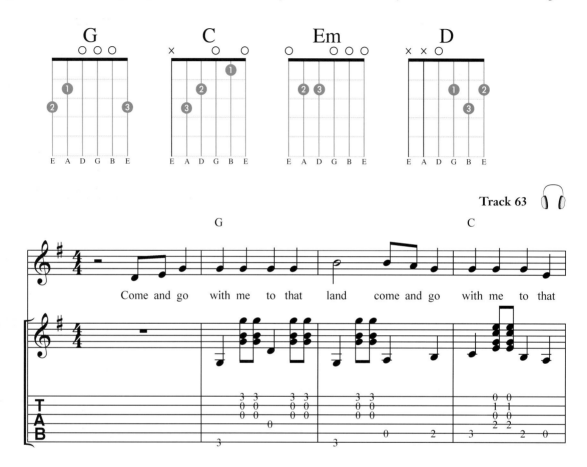

Track 63

Come and go   with me   to that   land   come and go   with me   to that

3/4 Timing

Not every song is in 4/4 timing. Most are, but you'll also come across a lot of songs in 3/4 timing, where each measure of music has three beats instead of four. Waltzes, such as "Mr. Bojangles" and "Piano Man" are good examples.

Ease into learning 3/4 rhythms by starting out with full chords played in straight quarter notes, eighth notes, or a mix of both:

Track 64

Now try the same thing, but this time substitute a single strike of the chord's root note for the first beat:

Track 65

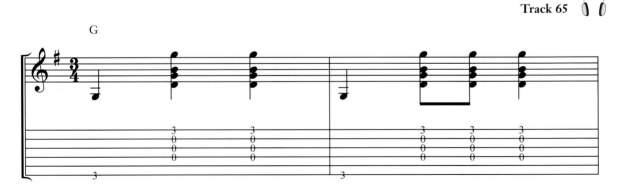

Now try adding an alternating bass pattern to 3/4 timing:

A very cool 3/4 strum uses a pair of eighth notes on the first beat and quarter notes on the second and third beats.

To get a smooth, fluid strum, be sure to hit the second eighth note as an upstroke. Try this C to G progression, first using a simple "bass/strum" and then using an alternating bass:

Track 67

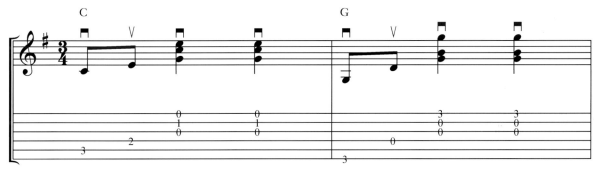

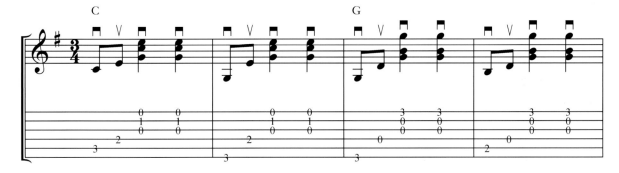

Slash Chords

Occasionally, a songwriter wants a note other than the root note to be the bass note of a chord. He may want a different note of the chord or even a note that's not a part of the chord. This would be indicated in the music by a slash chord.

With slash chords, the desired chord is on the left side of the slash ("/") and the new bass note is on the right. For example, "C/G" means that you want a C chord but you want the lowest G note possible to be the chord's bass note.

Here are some examples of slash chords you're likely to come across in music:

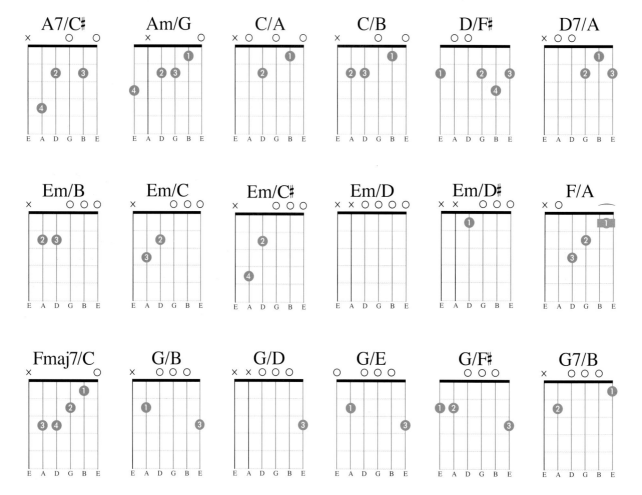

Pete Townshend often used slash chords to provide a single steady, droning bass note underneath a set of chord changes. In the following example, be sure to strum only the middle four strings of the guitar:

Track 68

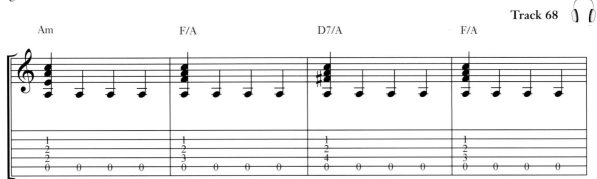

Slash chords are sometimes used as a step connecting two chords. Instead of simply switching from C to Am in the following example, adding the slash chord G/B between the C and Am makes the chord progression more interesting:

Track 69

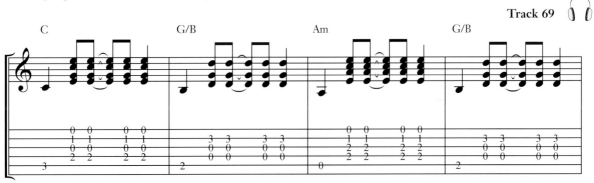

The most common use of slash chords is when the song keeps a chord the same while using a line of descending bass notes:

Track 70

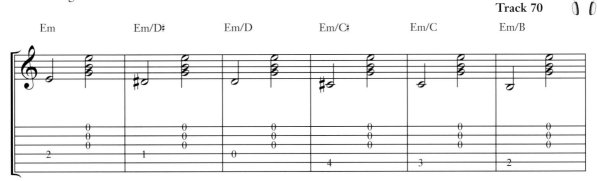

Practice: Slash Chords

And here are some examples in 3/4 time that you'll be using in the upcoming song, "Goodbye Old Paint."

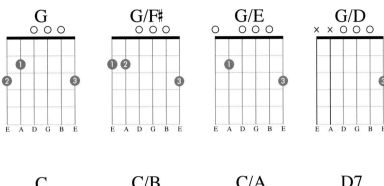

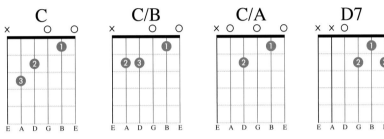

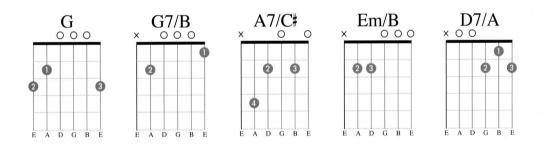

Practice: 3/4 Time and Slash Chords

The descending bass line of "Goodbye Old Paint" creates many of the slash chords you just learned. Plus, it offers a chance to practice strumming in 3/4 time.

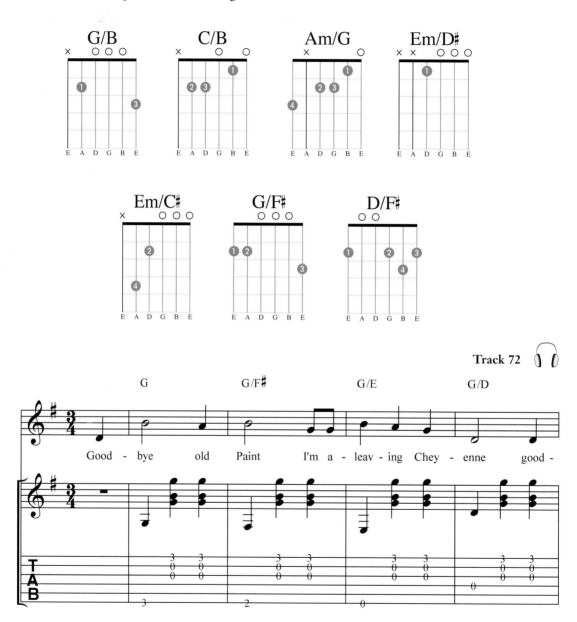

Track 72

Part 4

Growing Beyond the Beginner Stage

Once you're comfortable with basic chords and keeping a good, steady rhythm, you can start learning some techniques that will make you sound like you've been playing all your life!

This section will teach you simple and essential guitar nuances, such as percussive strumming and hammer-ons and pull-offs, that will add a lot of dynamic variation to your playing and sound way cooler than just your everyday basic strumming. And you'll also get an introduction to fingerstyle guitar playing!

Half-Barre Chords

All the chords you've learned so far are known as "open position" chords (also known as "cowboy chords") because they involve using notes of the open strings. Open position chords are easy for beginners, but there are many, many more chords for you to learn.

Barring is the first step toward exploring all the chords you can make up and down the neck of your guitar. To create a barre, you'll place a finger (usually the index finger) across a number of strings on the same fret. Covering all six strings with your finger is called a "full barre" and covering any other number of strings (from two to five) is called a "half barre."

You want to ease into barring by starting with half-barre chords such as these:

 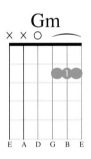 

 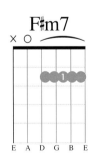 

After practicing these for a while, try your hand at an F major chord:

F

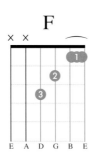

This will take some practice on your part, so don't get discouraged. The F chord is the nemesis of almost every beginning guitarist!

You can, in a pinch, use Fmaj7 as a substitute while you're working on perfecting the F chord:

Fmaj7

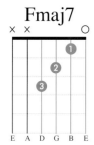

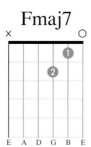

Try to keep your index finger parallel to the fret when forming a barre. Some guitarists find it helpful to feel the edge of the fret along the body side of the finger. Successful barres are about finger position, and not about pressure. The tip of your index finger should be at the edge of the last string you want to cover, and not extending beyond the upper edge of the guitar's neck.

Practice: Half-Barre Chords

Changing from open position chords to half-barre chords (and back) takes a little getting used to. These exercises, some of which involve alternating bass patterns and/or walking bass lines, will give you a good introduction to playing half-barre chords.

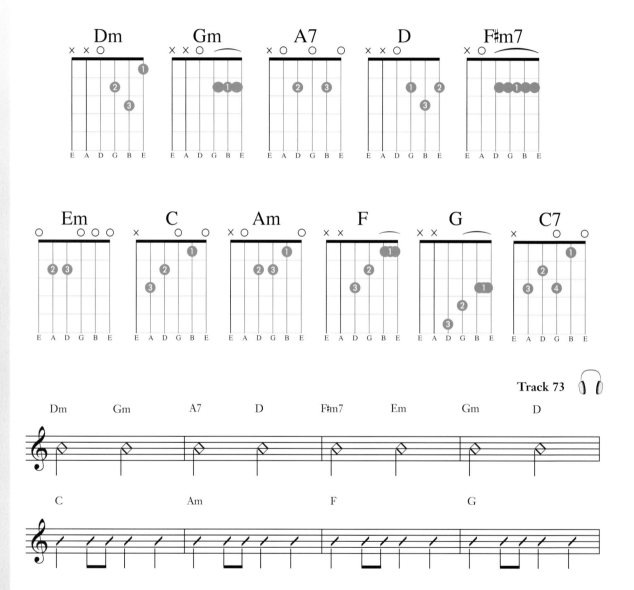

With many half barre chords, you will want to think ahead and use your index finger to cover one or more strings than you need for the current chord. The less you have to adjust your index finger, the smoother the chord change will usually be.

Practice: Song with F Chord

"Home Sweet Home" works you in easily with the new F chord. Should you find it too difficult at first, try using Fmaj7.

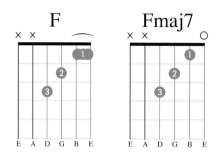

Track 74

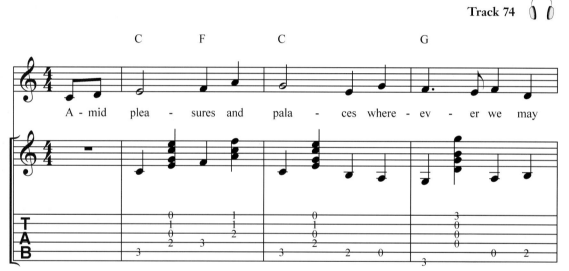

Percussive Strumming and String Muting

Your guitar is a one-man band sometimes, providing not only chords for a song's accompaniment but also the bass parts and even a bit of the drums! Learning to incorporate a bit of percussive strumming into your playing will make your rhythms more interesting, not to mention more fun.

Your right hand and left hand each have separate roles when it comes to playing percussively. With the right hand, you can perform a percussive stroke or palm muting.

To make a percussive stroke, bring the heel of your hand down on the strings (almost like a right-angle karate chop close to the saddle) at the same time you make a downstroke with your fingers or pick.

For palm muting, keep the heel of your right hand on your guitar strings close to the saddle *as* you pick the strings.

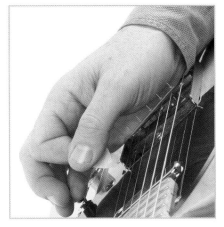

You can vary the tone of the muting by using more or less pressure on the strings.

Left Hand String Muting

The left hand takes care of string muting on the neck in one of two ways:

The simplest string muting technique is to just lay a finger (or all four fingers) lightly enough across all six strings to keep them from ringing when you strum.

Simply raising your fingers lightly off a chord and laying them slightly flatter to deaden adjoining strings is another effective way to create string muting.

In standard notation, rhythm notation, and guitar tablature, both percussive strokes and string muting are indicated either by ×-shaped note heads or an × in place of a number on the tablature staff. Here are a few samples to practice:

Track 75

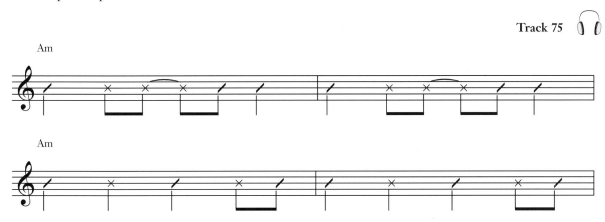

Practice: Palm Muting

Now try some simple palm muting:

Track 76

And here are more examples using both left and right hand muting:

Track 77

If you use a lot of arm motion to pick the strings, you will find palm muting to be a bit of a challenge. It's important to keep the heel of your hand relatively still and to let most of the picking motion come from your wrist and thumb.

Practice: Percussive Strumming Techniques

You'll get a lot of practice with both palm muting and percussive strumming with this arrangement of "Nobody Knows the Trouble I've Seen."

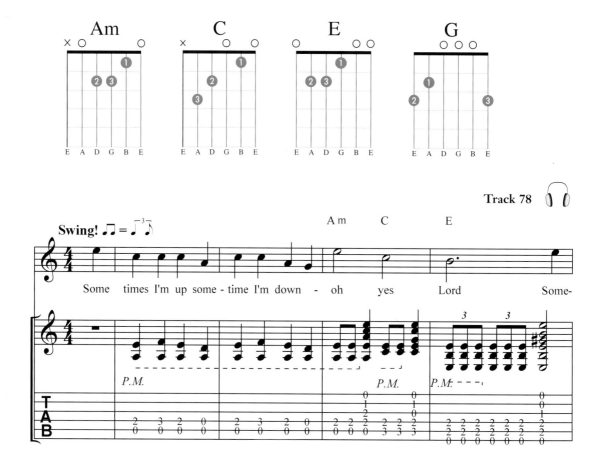

Track 78

Playing Arpeggios

You can also enhance your guitar playing with arpeggios, which is playing the notes of a chord string by string instead of strumming them all at once. The term *arpeggio* comes from the Italian for "to play like a harp" and, indeed, playing in this style gives the guitar a very harplike quality.

You can play arpeggios either with a pick or with your fingers. Here is a sample of what you can do with a G chord:

Track 79

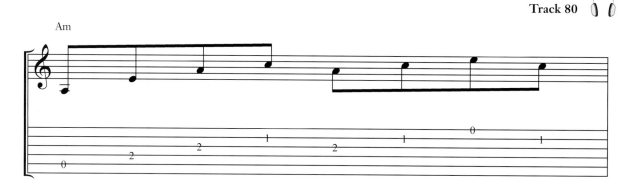

Now try an Am chord:

Track 80

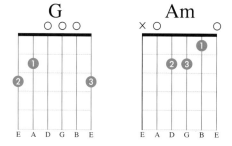

Playing arpeggios is a great way to check on how well you're doing fingering chords. Striking each string one at a time, you'll definitely hear it when your fingers aren't fretting a note properly or when they're brushing against adjacent strings. Take the time to play every chord you know as an arpeggio in order to take stock of how well you're fretting your chords at this point in your guitar playing. Also work on shifting from one chord to another.

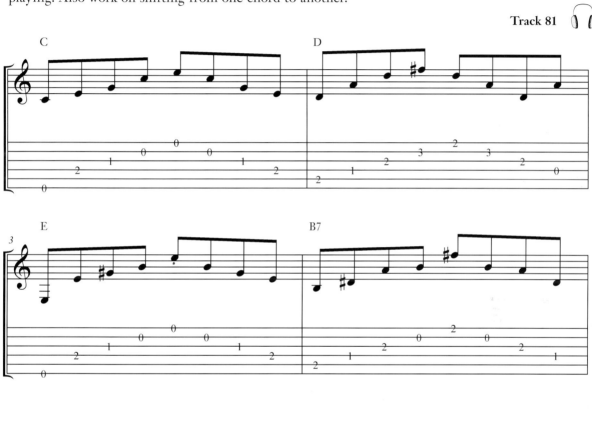

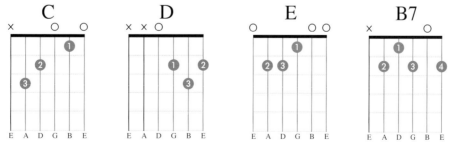

Practice: Arpeggios with Chords Aadd9 and E7

Arpeggios play a big part in creating very cool-sounding patterns when you combine them with a new *voicing* of chords you already know, such as these:

Aadd9

E7

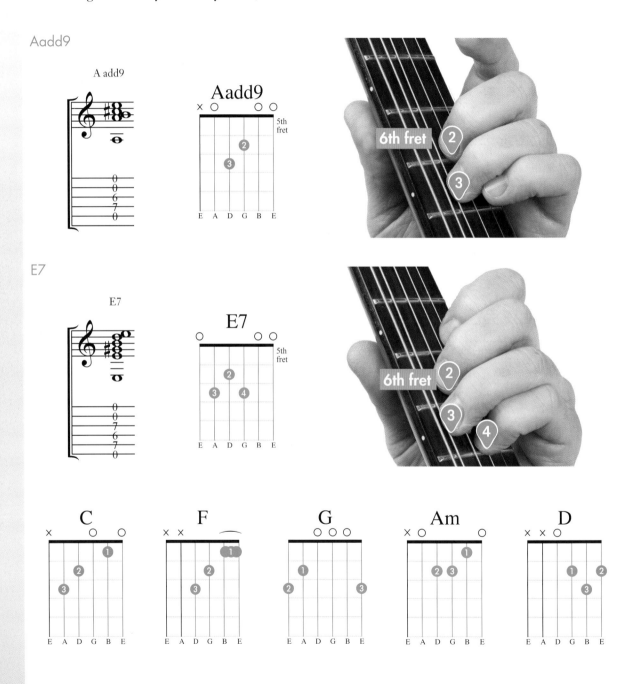

As you're going through all the chords you know, also be sure to try them in both 4/4 and 3/4 timing:

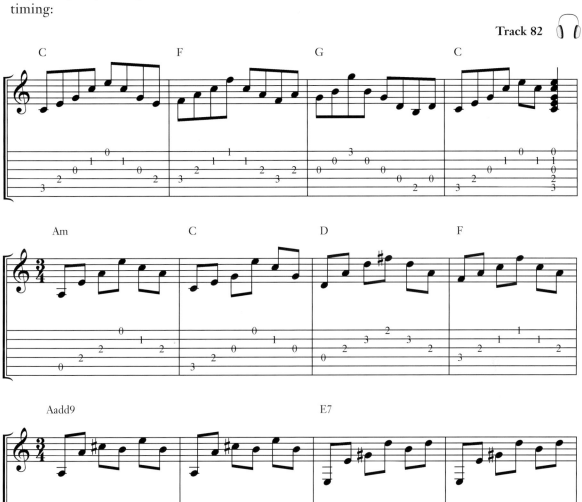

Practice: Songs with Arpeggios

You get the chance to use those two new chords (Aadd9 and the new voicing of E7) in this arrangement of "Down in the Valley," which is in 3/4 time:

Track 83

This arrangement of "The Old Grey Mare," which is played in a minor key, will probably sound a lot different than you remember the song. It also uses an alternating bass.

Track 84

Basic Fingerpicking

Playing the guitar in *fingerstyle*, also known as *fingerpicking*, may seem complicated, but it's actually quite easy to learn and a lot of fun to play. It's not difficult at all to pick up a few fingerpicking patterns and, better still, even a few simple picking patterns can make a song sound stunning.

It's best to start out simply by targeting strings for each finger of the right hand to pick:

Track 85

Keep your right arm relaxed and positioned so that the thumb and each finger can easily strike the strings.

Try to keep all your fingers off the face of the guitar. Some guitarists use the pinky to anchor the hand, and while this is acceptable, it can impede a smooth picking motion.

Keep your right arm relaxed and positioned so that the thumb and each finger can easily strike the strings.

You can pick the strings with either your nails or the pads of the fingers. Both choices produce different tones. If you go with your nails, you will want to spend time filing and shaping them, and you may also decide to use lacquer or some other clear coating to keep them strong.

In the following examples, try as much as possible to follow the fingerpicking guides. "P" is your thumb, "i" the index finger, "m" the middle finger, and "a" the ring finger.

Track 86

Practice: Two Easy Classical Studies

These two pieces by Ferdinando Carulli are a great introduction to the world of classical guitar music. "Caprice" is based around the chords G, D7, and C:

Track 87

The second piece is "Waltz" (played in 3/4 time), which centers around the A chord:

Introduction to Travis-Style Fingerpicking

Travis-style fingerpicking is a style of fingerpicking that involves alternating your picking between the thumb and the fingers. It's named after Merle Travis, a superb guitarist of the early and middle part of the last century. Basic Travis-style fingerpicking is the basis of most of the fingerstyle music you hear.

And it's very easy to pick up the basics. Start with an Am chord and use your thumb ("p") to alternately pick the A and D strings on the beat:

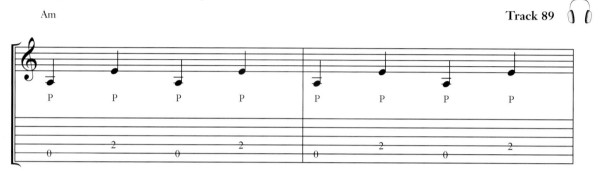

Then, using your middle finger ("m") on the B string and your index finger ("i") on the G string, fill in the eighth notes between the beats:

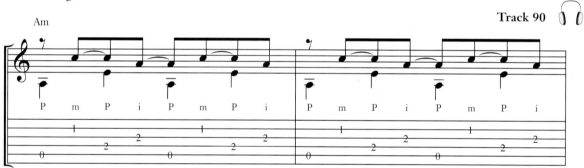

You can also try out different patterns:

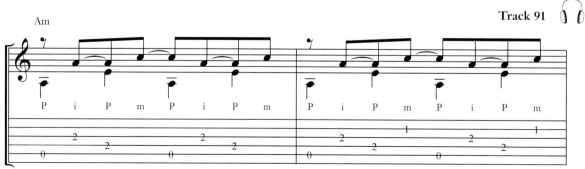

When you feel confident with these examples, try replacing the first beat with a "pinch," a simultaneous pick of two strings using both the thumb and appropriate finger:

Here are a few exercises using Travis-style fingerpicking that involve changing chords as well. Take your time practicing these in order to get the proper picking and correct rhythms.

Track 92

Practice: Basic Travis-Style Fingerpicking

Even though "Mockingbird" uses only two chords, this arrangement changes keys twice, giving you the opportunity to use your basic Travis-style fingerpicking pattern on six different chords:

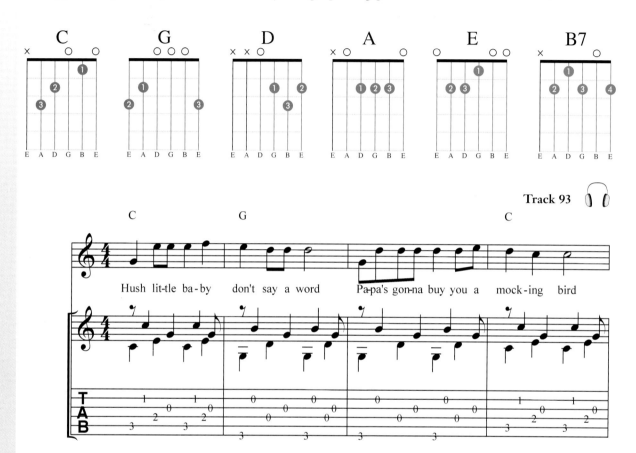

Practice: Basic Travis-Style Fingerpicking with Pinching

Don't obsess over following the music to this arrangement of "The Yellow Rose of Texas" exactly note for note. You're going to miss strings here and there in the pattern, but as long as you're holding on to the full chord while playing and you maintain a steady beat, you'll be fine!

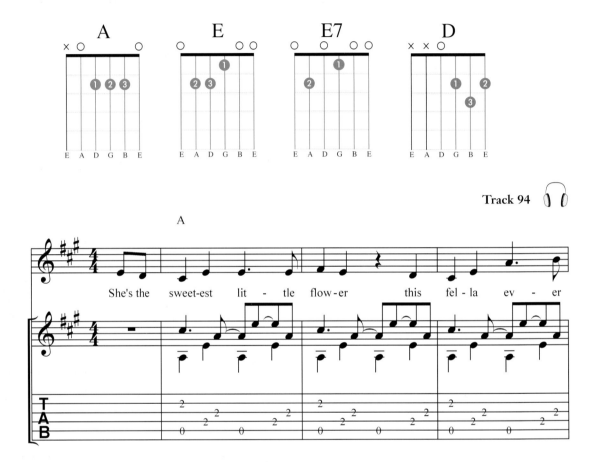

Track 94

Hammer-ons and Pull-offs

You may notice that many guitarists' left hands seem to be as busy as the right when playing. They're often using *slurs*, four techniques in which the left hand is responsible for producing notes on its own. *Hammer-ons* and *pull-offs* are two of these four basic slur techniques.

To perform a hammer-on:

Position finger 1 above the second fret of the D string. Pick the open string with the right hand and then bring finger 1 down in a fast, hard motion onto the second fret of the D string. Hit it square with the fingertip and keep it there just as you would when normally fretting a note.

Track 95

For a pull-off:

Place finger 3 at the third fret of the high E string and then pick the string with the right hand. After the note sounds, give finger 3 a downward tug off the string. Don't lift the finger straight off—the tugging will sound the note of the open high E string.

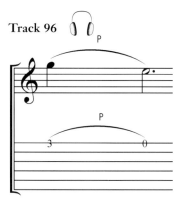

Track 96

You can also use hammer-ons and pull-offs in succession:

Place finger 1 on the first fret of your B string. Keep it firmly in place while performing a hammer-on onto the third fret of the B string with finger 3. With finger 1 still in place, perform a pull-off at the third fret of the B string with finger 3.

Track 97

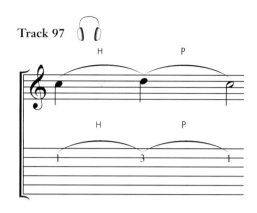

Be sure to follow the correct timing when it comes to hammer-ons, pull-offs, and other slurs. A *grace note* indicates to play the slur as quickly as you can to get onto the beat.

Track 98

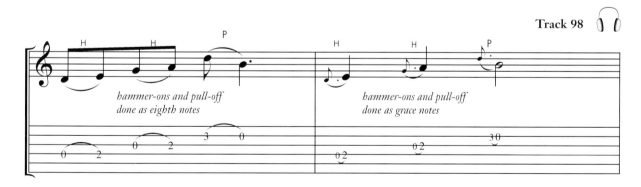

hammer-ons and pull-off done as eighth notes

hammer-ons and pull-off done as grace notes

Strumming and Picking Hammer-ons and Pull-offs

Mixing slurs like hammer-ons and pull-offs with all the strumming techniques and picking styles you already know takes your playing to a whole new level. Here are some examples to get you started. Be sure to experiment and try out ideas of your own.

Track 99

Practice: Hammer-ons and Pull-offs

This arrangement of "Hard Ain't It Hard" will give you a good workout with hammer-ons and pull-offs.

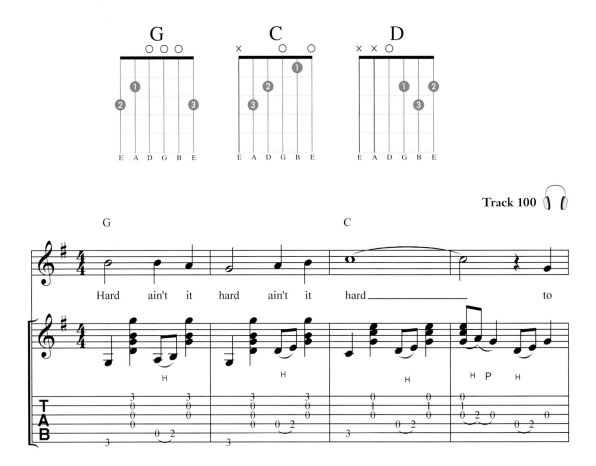

Slides and Bends

Slides and *bends* are the other two of the four basic slur techniques. Both will require some practice and patience on your part.

Slides, especially, seem very easy. You want to let your finger glide along the same string on the fretboard from one note to another. This requires a good sense of touch on the strings.

Place finger 3 on the second fret of the G string and then pick the string with the right hand. Ease the pressure on the string lightly enough to slide finger 3 from the second fret to the fourth fret. Too much pressure and you'll never make it over the intervening frets. Too little pressure and you'll lose the sound of the slide. Once you've arrived at the fourth fret, reapply pressure to the string to sustain the new note.

You can slide along several strings as well as a single string. And sliding is also an excellent way to reposition your fingers at a different place on the neck, which will come in handy when you learn about fills later on.

Track 101

Bending a string raises the initial pitch of the original note. The secret to bending is to use your wrist for the motion and not try to push the string across the neck solely with the fingers. You may find it easier to do your first bends with two or three fingers on the same string.

Place finger 3 on the eighth fret of your B string (you may also want to place fingers 1 and 2 on the seventh fret of the B string for assistance). Using a wrist motion similar to turning a key in an ignition, let finger 3 shift to the lower side of the B string and push it toward the center of the neck. Try to push the string *parallel* to the neck and not *into* it.

Bending requires you to be able to hear your targeted pitch. Depending on the strength of your bend, you can raise the initial notes a musical half-step (the equivalent of one fret) or full-step (two frets) higher. A slight bend will result in a slight raising of pitch, less than a half-step. This "quarter bend" technique is used often in blues guitar playing.

Practice: Slides and Bends

Here are some exercises using all four of the slur techniques you've learned:

Track 103

Practice: All Four Slurs

"Hand Me Down My Walking Cane" is the trickiest song you've attempted so far. Work through this arrangement phrase by phrase until you're comfortable about putting the whole song together.

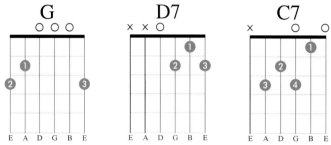

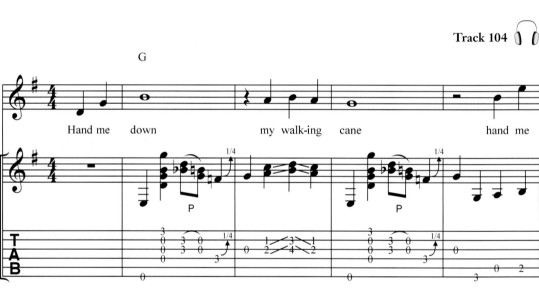

Part 5

Adding Theory to Your Playing

It's time to put all the techniques you've learned to good use! With the help of a little basic music theory, you'll soon be playing chords all up and down the neck of your guitar. You'll also learn how to use a capo and transpose, as well as explore various tunings on your guitar.

Plus, you'll get tips on how to create fills and how to improvise solos, all of which adds more depth to your playing. And you'll learn how to play with other musicians, which is one of the most fun ways to learn even more about music and the guitar.

The Major Scale

Scales are a defined series of notes, beginning with the chosen root note and then going through a specific combination of musical steps and half-steps until you reach the next occurrence of the root note.

A *chromatic scale*, for example, starts with a given note and then goes to each successive note in half-steps until you reach the root note once more. Here is the A chromatic scale:

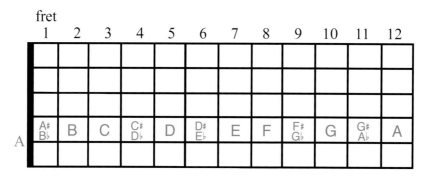

Everything you want to know about chords is connected to the *major scale*, which you probably know as the "Do, re, mi" scale from *The Sound of Music*.

To create the major scale, pick a root note and then follow this pattern of whole steps ("W") and half-steps ("H"):

Root   W   W   H   W   W   W   H (the root note again)

Now that you have the pattern, create the C major scale:

C   D   E   F   G   A   B   C

Then try the G major scale. When you get to E, remember the next note is a whole step higher, so you will use F♯ and not F, which is only a half-step higher than E:

G   A   B   C   D   E   F♯   G

Intervals

The distance from any one note to another is called an *interval*. Intervals are given generic numbers based on the major scale. Using the C major scale as an example:

1	2	3	4	5	6	7	8
C	D	E	F	G	A	B	C

C to D = major second   C to D♭ = minor second

C to E = major third   C to E♭ = minor third

C to F = perfect fourth

C to G = perfect fifth   C to G♭ = diminished fifth

C to A = major sixth   C to A♭ = minor sixth

C to B = major seventh   C to B♭ = flat seventh

C to C = octave

You also want to know that the interval of the minor sixth (C to A♭ in this example) is often thought of as being the interval of C to G♯, which is referred to as the "augmented fifth."

Finding the Major Scale All Over the Neck

Scales will be important to know when you work on playing fills and improvising solos. Here is the G major scale, played through two octaves, first using open strings and then using no open strings, which is called a *closed position* scale pattern:

G major scale (open)

G major scale (closed)

Knowing this closed position scale pattern means you can play any major scale you want to, anywhere on the neck, as long as you know where your root note is on the low E string.

How Chords Are Formed

With your knowledge of chords and intervals, you can now create any chord possible. In Western music, chords are based on *triads*, which are notes separated by the interval of a third. It can either be a major third or a minor third. Using the key of D as an example, write out the D major scale:

D	E	F♯	G	A	B	C♯	D

Starting with the root note, D, you would also take the F♯ (the third) and the A (the fifth, which is a third above the third), and you would have a D major chord.

There are four basic chords, each based on using the root, third, and fifth of the major scale. But three of the chords use different intervals between the notes. If you remember that there are two types of thirds (major and minor) and that the interval between the third and the fifth is also a third, then you can use the four possible combinations of major and minor thirds to create the four basic types of chords:

Major	=	Root	+	Major third	+	Minor third
Minor	=	Root	+	Minor third	+	Major third
Augmented	=	Root	+	Major third	+	Major third
Diminished	=	Root	+	Minor third	+	Minor third

Now try out each of these chords and listen to their particular tonal qualities:

D Major

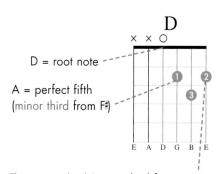

D = root note

A = perfect fifth
(minor third from F♯)

F♯ = major third (major third from root)

D Minor

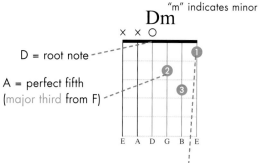

"m" indicates minor

D = root note

A = perfect fifth
(major third from F)

F = minor third (minor third from root)

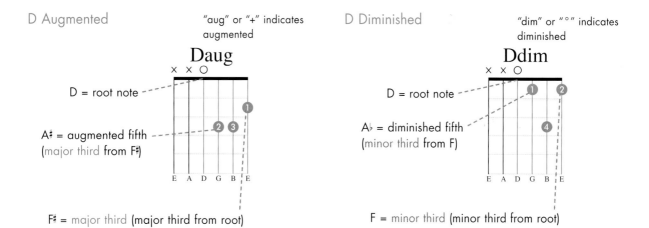

"aug" or "+" indicates augmented

Daug

x x o

D = root note

A# = augmented fifth
(major third from F#)

E   A   D   G   B   E

F# = major third (major third from root)

D Diminished

"dim" or "°" indicates diminished

Ddim

x x o

D = root note

A♭ = diminished fifth
(minor third from F)

E   A   D   G   B   E

F = minor third (minor third from root)

It should be noted that the vast majority of chords you'll run across in music will be either major or minor, or some variation of the major or minor chords, such as those you'll learn about in the following pages.

Adding Other Notes

Once you have your basic chord, be it major, minor, augmented, or diminished, you may also add other notes to it. These chords are indicated by placing a number after the basic chord, such as "C7," "Em7," "D9," and so on. The numbers refer to a note's place in the major scale of the root note. "D6," for example, means you want to add the sixth note of the D major scale, which is B, to the D chord, like this:

D6

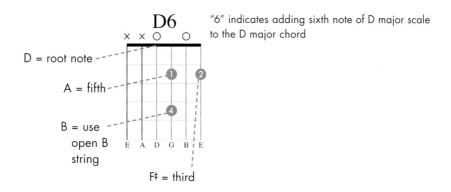

D6

x x o   o

"6" indicates adding sixth note of D major scale to the D major chord

D = root note

A = fifth

B = use
open B
string

E   A   D   G   B   E

F# = third

Power Chords and Suspended Chords

Power chords, also known as "5" chords, are not technically chords at all. They are simply the root note and fifth note of the major scale played together. 5 chords sound neither major nor minor, since they have no third. They are used extensively in rock music, as they sound very cool on electric guitars with the distortion cranked up on the amplifier.

A5   D5   D5 (four note version)

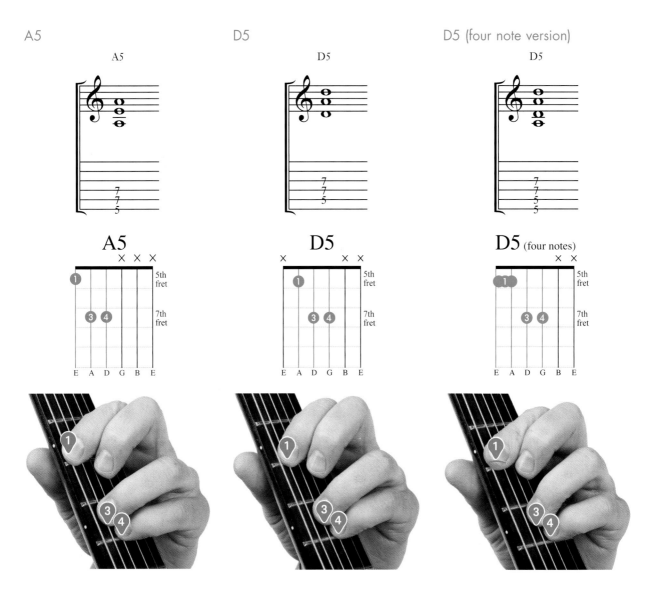

Suspended Chords

In suspended chords (also known as "sus" chords for short), such as the Asus2, Dsus2, and Esus4 you learned earlier, the third is replaced by either the second or the fourth note of the scale. If a chord reads simply "sus," such as Gsus, assume that the fourth is going to be the substitute for the third.

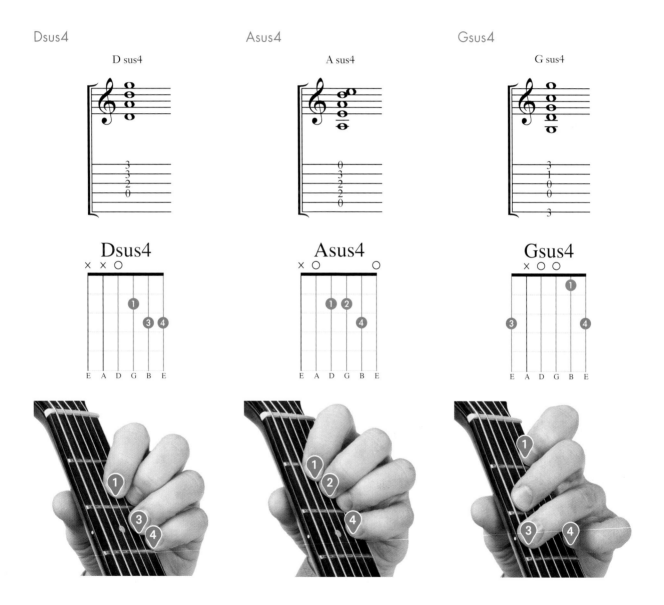

Practice: Various 5 Chords and Suspended Chords

Think of this arrangement of "The Erie Canal" as a two-part exercise. You will use a number of 5 chords in the verses of the song and then switch to using suspended chords in the chorus.

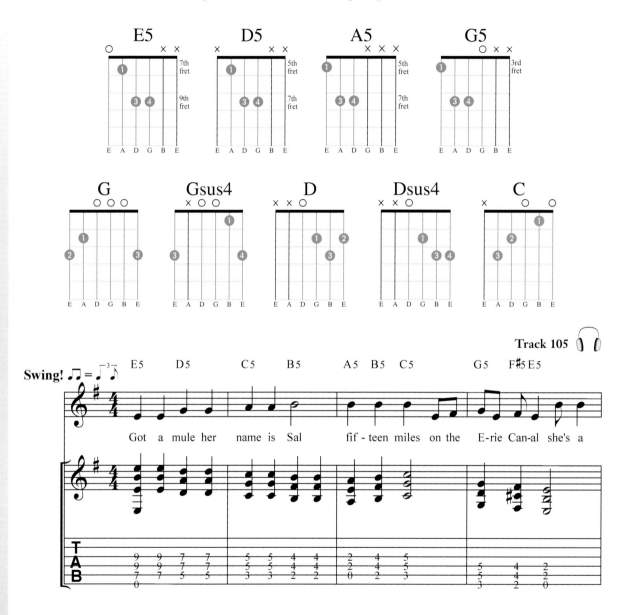

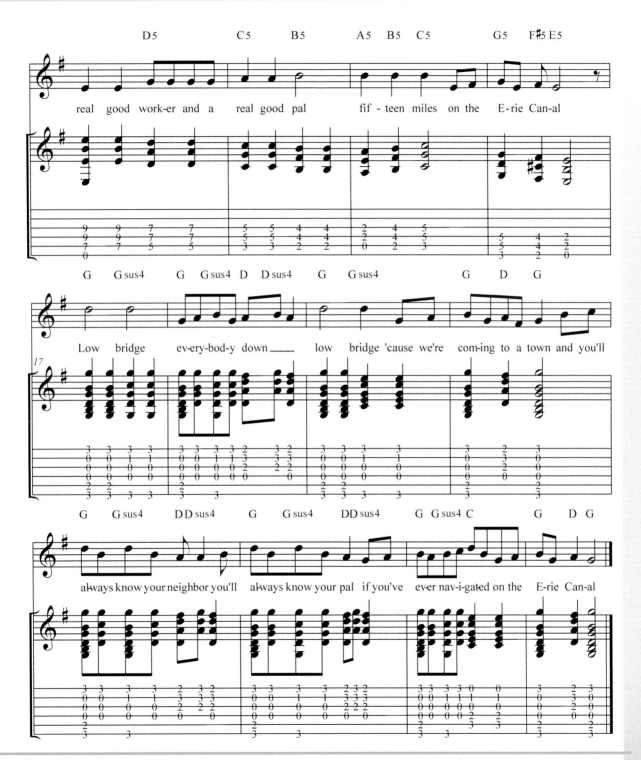

Seventh Chords

There are many types of seventh chords, and the way they're formed can initially seem confusing.

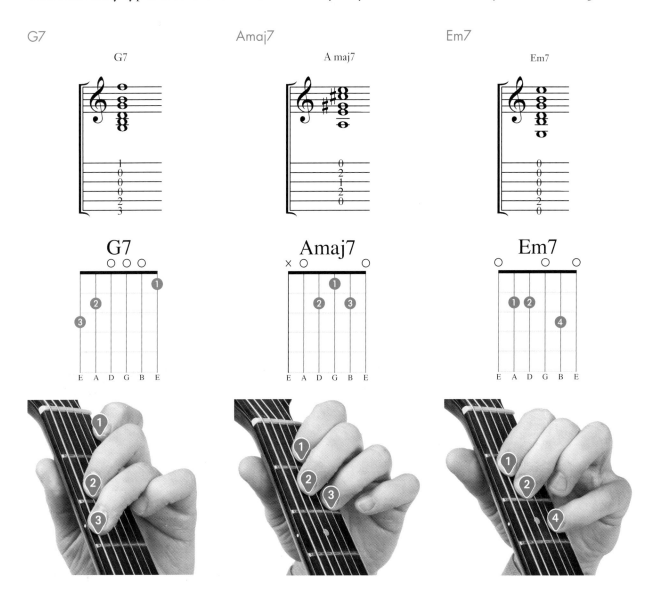

Whenever you see just "7" it means to add the interval of the flat seven to the basic chord. 7 chords are also called "dominant sevenths."

"maj7," short for "major seventh," means to add the interval of the major seven to the basic chord. A good way to remember this is that whenever you see the word "major" tacked onto a chord name, it's always referring to the seventh, just as an "m" for "minor" always refers to the third.

Again, the "m" for minor refers to the basic chord. The "7" indicates a dominant seventh, so you want to add the interval of the flat seventh (D in this case) to the Em chord.

And here are some more seventh chords to practice:

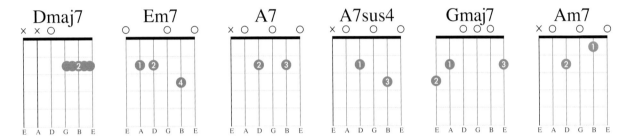

Here are some exercises involving various types of seventh chords:

Track 106

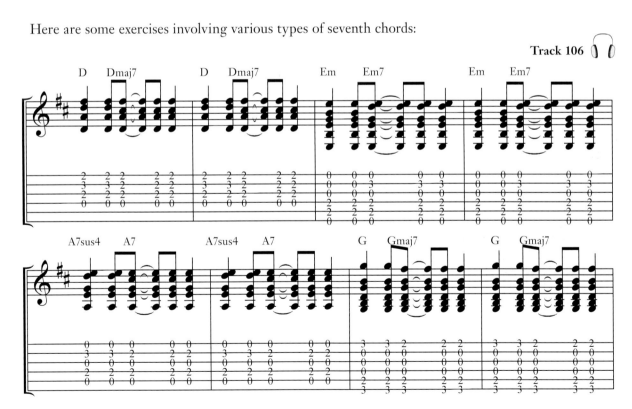

Practice: Various Seventh Chords

This arrangement of "The Banks of the Ohio" mimics the style of "Everybody's Talking" from the movie *Midnight Cowboy*. Be careful of the syncopation used in the strumming.

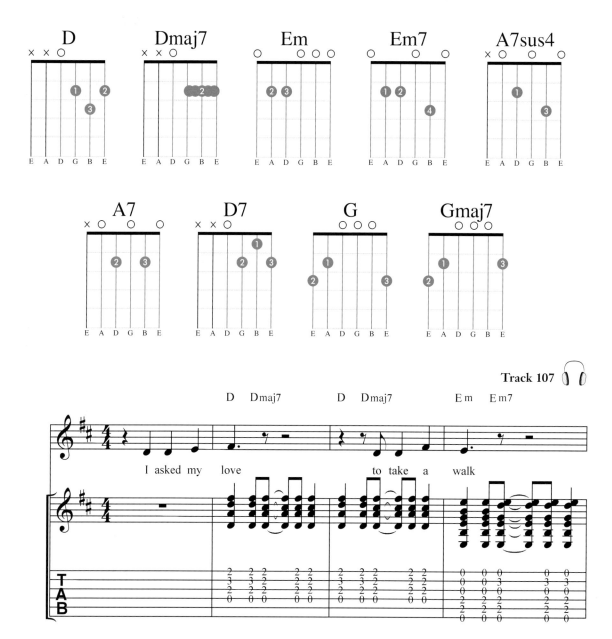

Track 107

Really Fancy Chords

As a beginner, it's easy to be intimidated by complicated chords. Remember that the root note is "1" and also "8" at the octave and that any note higher than 8 is a repeat of one you already know. In the key of C, for example, your notes would repeat like this:

1	2	3	4	5	6	7
C	D	E	F	G	A	B
	9		11		13	

You won't see the numbers 8, 10, and 12 because they are already part of the basic C chord. When you get past 8, you will either see "add9," which means to add just the D note to the rest of the C chord (C, E, and G), or "C9," which indicates you want to also have the dominant seventh as part of the chord. "Maj9" would mean you'd want to use the major seventh instead of the dominant seventh.

Here's a handy chart to help you:

"add9"	Root	3rd	5th	9th		
"9"	Root	3rd	5th	♭7th	9th	
"maj9"	Root	3rd	5th	major 7th	9th	
"11"	Root	3rd	5th	♭7th	9th	11th
"13"	Root	3rd	5th	♭7th	9th	11th	13th

C9

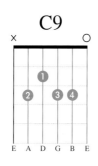

C9

A13

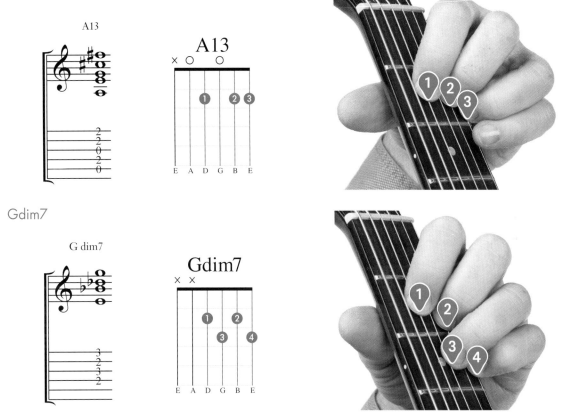

Gdim7

Here are some more fancy chords for you to practice:

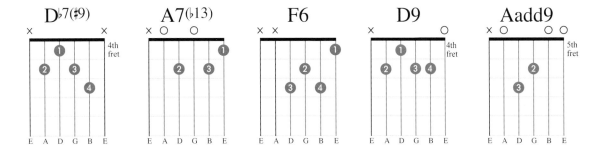

Whenever you run into a chord you're not sure of, feel free to substitute a basic chord for it. "A13" can be replaced by A or A7. "Em11" would be substituted by Em or Em7. If the chord name indicates any changes to the 5, such as "G7♯5," remember that ♯5 is an augmented chord, while ♭5 is a diminished one.

Practice: Various Fancy Chords

Take your time with this arrangement of "Fancy Chord Waltz." While the chords may seem intimidating, they are all within your capabilities. Practice changing between each chord before taking on the whole piece.

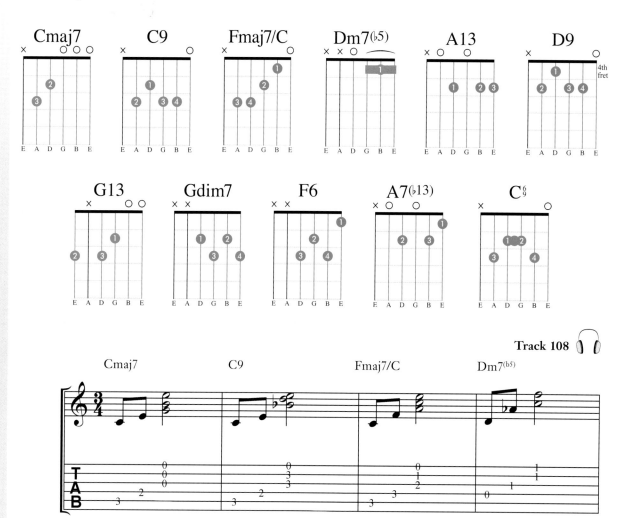

Full Barre Chords

Full barre chords require you to use your index finger to barre across all six strings. Now that you have a lot of experience with all types of chords, you'll probably find them a little easier than you would have when you learned half-barre chords. Start out with barre chords that use the shapes of E, Em, and E7:

A (full barre)

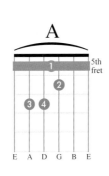

Index finger lies flat across all six strings at the fifth fret while other fingers form the shape of an E chord.

Am (full barre)

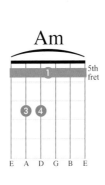

Index finger lies flat across all six strings at the fifth fret while other fingers form the shape of an Em chord.

A7 (full barre)

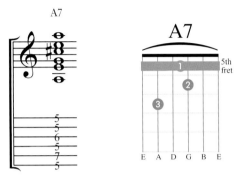

Index finger lies flat across all six strings at the fifth fret while other fingers form the shape of an E7 chord.

Now try these A-shaped barre chords:

D (full barre)

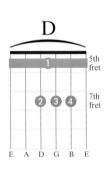

Index finger lies flat across all six strings at the fifth fret while other fingers form the shape of an A chord.

Many guitarists have a hard time with this particular barre chord shape. Instead, they barre the ring finger at the seventh fret (still playing the fifth fret of the A string with the index finger) and don't strum all the way through to the high E string.

Full Barre Chords (continued)

Dm (full barre)

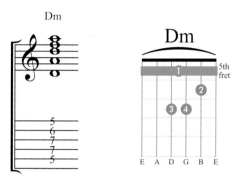

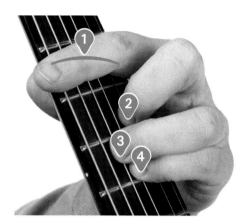

Index finger lies flat across all six strings at the fifth fret while other fingers form the shape of an Am chord.

Dm7 (full barre)

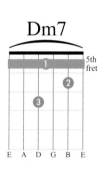

Index finger lies flat across all six strings at the fifth fret while other fingers form the shape of an Am7 chord.

Here is a full barre chord where your fingers form a C chord:

F (full barre)

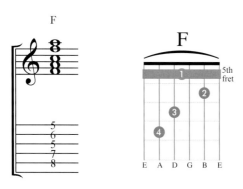

Index finger lies flat across all six strings at the fifth fret while other fingers form the shape of a C chord.

Even more guitarists have a hard time with the C-shaped barre chord and will often just play the four thinnest strings of the chord, much like the Am7-shaped barre that you just learned.

You can often substitute a C7 or C9 closed position chord for a C-shaped barre chord. If you're playing a full barre A chord with an E shape at the fifth fret and your next chord is an E (normally a C-shaped full barre at the fourth fret), try either of these as a substitute:

E7 (C7 non-barre)

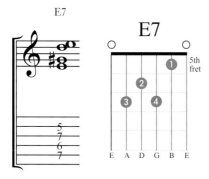

E9 (C9 non-barre)

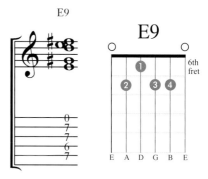

This closed position C9 shape is used very frequently in jazz, blues, and funk music. Keep the ring finger parallel to the fret and be sure to arch your middle finger in order to keep the note on the D string from being muted.

Practice: Full Barre Chords

To make your first full song with barre chords a little easier, this arrangement of "Bury Me Beneath the Willow" uses only three chords. Not only are just two of them barre chords, but you also get to stay in one position on the neck.

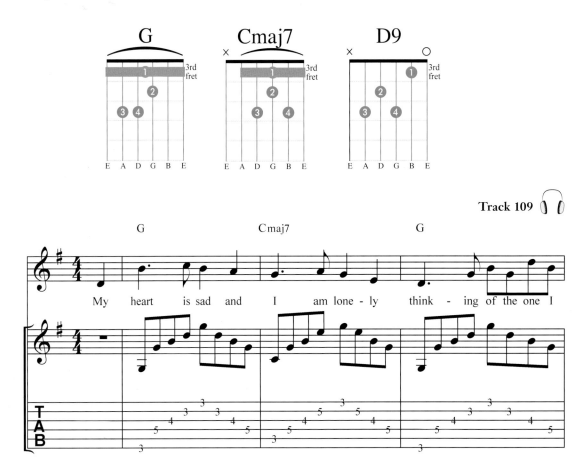

Creating Different Chord Voicings

When you learned "Down in the Valley" as part of the lesson on arpeggios, you got a taste of using the open strings of the guitar to create mesmerizing new chords. Now that you have a bit of music theory and chord knowledge, you can take that a huge step further.

Fancy G

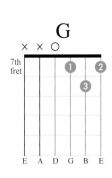

Form an open position D chord at the seventh and eighth frets. You can play the open D string as if it's part of the chord.

Fancy D

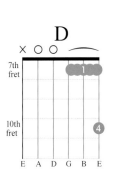

Barre the first three strings at the seventh fret and then place your little finger at the tenth fret. You can play both the open D and open A strings.

Fancy E9

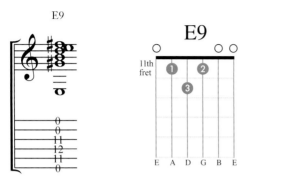

E9

11th fret

E A D G B E

Place finger 1 on the eleventh fret of the A string, finger 3 on the twelfth fret of the D string, and finger 2 on the eleventh fret of the G string and strum across all six strings.

The secret to using different chord voicings is to play them so often that you automatically think of them as regular chords. Here are some exercises to help you get started:

Track 110

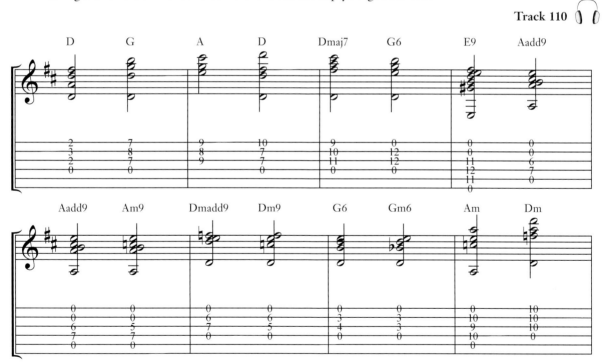

Practice: Various Chord Voicings

Learning new chord voicings is just the first step to advancing your knowledge of the fretboard. You also want to be able to change smoothly from one chord voicing to another, which comes from knowing where different chord voicings are in relation to each other.

This arrangement of "Danny Boy" involves many different chord voicings for the basic chords of D, G, E, and A. Each chord is played for four beats, except for the E9 and the Aadd9 in the next-to-last measure. Practice the changes of position slowly, measure by measure, to give yourself time to move from one section of the neck to another in the correct rhythm. Pay close attention to how each chord flows smoothly into the next with a minimal amount of finger movement.

Taking the extra step to listen to what you play and to understand how the chords relate to each other will be more beneficial to you as a guitarist and musician than simply following the tablature, or just reading the chord names. Many beginner guitarists fall into a "tablature mentality" where they only follow directions and copy what's played, instead of exploring the many possibilities their guitars can offer. See how many of these new chord voicings you can use in the other songs you've learned, and try to come up with more fancy chord voicings of your own.

Track 111

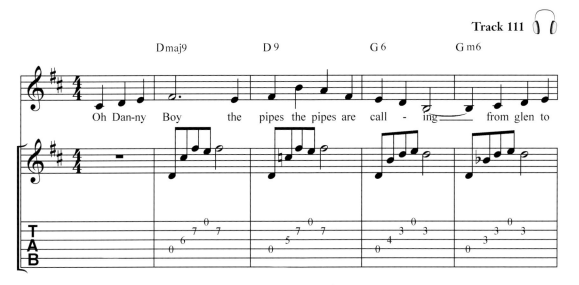

Keys, Key Signatures, and the Circle of Fifths

While there are many types of chords, it's rare for a song to use more than a handful of them. Knowing a little about keys and how chords are created within a given key can help you anticipate what chords are likely to show up in a song.

A song's *key* is its tonal center. It is often indicated by a song's *key signature*, which are the number of flats or sharps placed at the very left of a staff of music notation. There are twelve notes, so there are twelve possible keys and key signatures:

Key of C: C, D, E, F, G, A, B, C

Key of G: G, A, B, C, D, E, F#, G

Key of D: D, E, F#, G, A, B, C#, D

Key of A: A, B, C#, D, E, F#, G#, A

Key of E: E, F#, G#, A, B, C#, D#, E

Key of B: B, C#, D#, E, F#, G#, A#, B

Key of F#: F#, G#, A#, B, C#, D#, E#, F#

Key of F: F, G, A, B♭, C, D, E, F

Key of B♭: B♭, C, D, E♭, F, G, A, B♭

Key of E♭: E♭, G, A♭, B♭, C, D, E♭

Key of A♭: A♭, B♭, C, D♭, E♭, F, G, A♭

Key of D♭: D♭, E, F#, G, A, B, C#, D♭

Circle of Fifths

A handy visual method of learning and remembering key signatures is the Circle of Fifths.

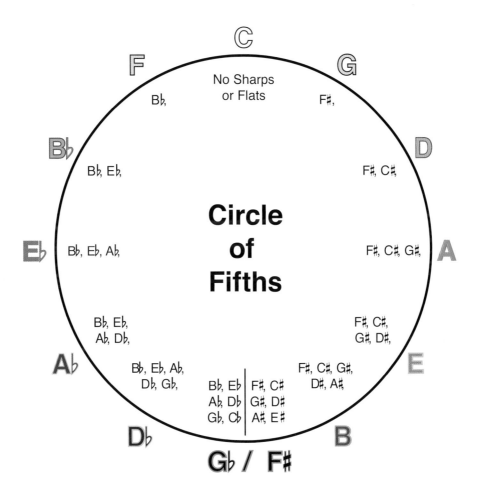

Think of the circle as an analog clock with the note of each of the twelve major keys at a different position on the clock's face. The scale of C major, at the twelve o'clock position, has no flats and no sharps. Moving clockwise, the next key, G major (at the one o'clock position), has one sharp in its scale (F♯). D major has two sharps (F♯ and C♯), A major has three, and so on until you get to the key of F♯ major (with six sharps) at the six o'clock position.

And since F♯ and G♭ are the same notes, you have completed your circle.

Diatonic Chords and Transposing

When you know the major scale of any key, you can then figure out the *diatonic chords* of that key. Diatonic means the chord uses only notes from the chosen key signature, so all the diatonic chords in the key of C major, for example, contain no flats or sharps. The diatonic chords of the key of G major may contain F♯ but won't ever have F natural.

To construct the diatonic chords of any key, first write out the key's major scale (try using C major as your first example). Then add the third and fifth notes up from your starting note. The entire process, in the key of C, will look like this:

Finding the Diatonic Chords in the Key of C

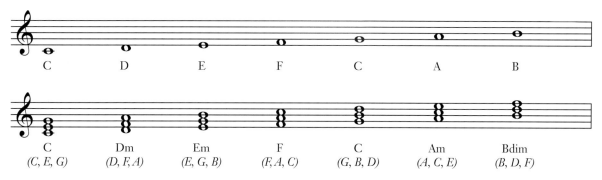

This pattern of chords—major, minor, minor, major, major, minor, and diminished—holds true for the major scale of every key. It's rare that you'll see the use of diminished chords, so focus on the first six chords.

> Roman numerals are usually used to generically denote diatonic triads of a key. Often the major chords (I, IV, and V) are capitalized, while the minor chords (ii, iii, and vi) are lowercase.
>
> For example, if someone tells you a song is in the key of C, the chords you're most likely to find in the song are C, F, and G (the I, IV, and V chords), as well as Dm, Em, and Am (the ii, iii, and vi chords).

Diatonic Chords in Every Key

I	ii	III	IV	V	vi
C	Dm	Em	F	G	Am
D♭	E♭m	Fm	G♭	A♭	B♭m
D	Em	F♯m	G	A	Bm
E♭	Fm	Gm	A♭	B♭	Cm
E	F♯m	G♯m	A	B	C♯m
F	Gm	Am	B♭	C	Dm
F♯	G♯m	A♯m	B	C♯	D♯m
G	Am	Bm	C	D	Em
A♭	B♭m	Cm	D♭	E♭	Fm
A	Bm	C♯m	D	E	F♯m
B♭	Cm	Dm	E♭	F	Gm
B	C♯m	D♯m	E	F♯	G♯m

Transposing

This knowledge of keys and diatonic chords allows you to *transpose* songs into different keys. Transposing is changing the notes and chords from one key to another.

Suppose you run across a song you like but the chords are difficult for you to play. For example, say the song in question is in the key of E♭ and uses the chords E♭, Cm, A♭, and B♭.

Looking at the chart of diatonic chords, you see that in the row for the key of E♭ (the key will be under the column marked "I"), these are the I, vi, IV, and V chords. Take a look at the other rows and see if there is a set of I, vi, IV, and V chords you would prefer to play. Chances are you'll like the chords in the key of C (C, Am, F, and G), the key of D (D, Bm, G, and A), and the key of G (G, Em, C, and D).

When transposing, focus on the root note of the chord and don't worry about how complicated a chord it might seem to be. You simply transfer all of the chord's "baggage" to the new root note. Suppose the chords in our last example were E♭, Cm7, A♭add9, and B♭sus4. In the key of C, that chord progression would transpose to C, Am7, Fadd9, and Gsus4.

Remember, too, that while many songs use only diatonic chords, you will often run into songs that borrow chords from other keys. If the Cm7 in the key of E♭ of the last example had been C7, that would have transposed to A7 in the key of C.

Using a Capo

A *capo* is a clamplike device you attach at a single fret on the neck of your guitar. Because it covers all six strings, you're raising the pitch of your guitar one half-step for each fret. If you put a capo on your third fret, for example, the open strings (low to high) are tuned to the notes G, C, F, B♭, D, and G. Likewise, every chord you know is also raised in pitch in respect to where you place the capo:

Capo chord chart

Capo on Fret:	1	2	3	4	5	6	7	8	9
Open Chord:									
A becomes	B♭	B	C	C♯	D	E♭	E	F	F♯
C becomes	C♯	D	E♭	E	F	F♯	G	G♯	A
D becomes	E♭	E	F	F♯	G	G♯	A	B♭	B
E becomes	F	F♯	G	G♯	A	B♭	B	C	C♯
F becomes	F♯	G	G♯	A	B♭	B	C	C♯	D
G becomes	G♯	A	B♭	B	C	C♯	D	E♭	E

Using a Capo

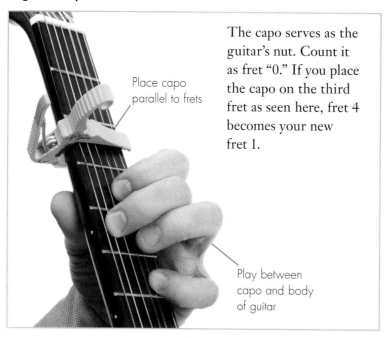

Place capo parallel to frets

Play between capo and body of guitar

The capo serves as the guitar's nut. Count it as fret "0." If you place the capo on the third fret as seen here, fret 4 becomes your new fret 1.

When you transpose a song to make it easier to play, using a capo can raise the song back to its original key while keeping the chords easy. Say you've taken a song in E♭ (with the chords E♭, A♭, and B♭) and transposed it down a half-step to D, where the chords are now D, G, and A. Placing the capo on the first fret raises each of those chords a half-step, giving you E♭, A♭, and B♭ even though to you it seems you're playing D, G, and A.

When you're playing with other guitarists, using a capo allows you to bring a different voice to the ensemble. Here is an example of two guitars playing together. "Guitar 1" is a regular guitar with no capo and "Guitar 2" has a capo on the seventh fret.

Track 112

Practice: Song for Two Guitars

The first of the two guitar parts ("Guitar 1") of this arrangement of "Will the Circle Be Unbroken" is a simple alternating bass/strumming part with a few walking bass lines for good measure. The "Guitar 2" part uses arpeggios as well as a few hammer-ons and pull-offs.

Practice: Song for Two Guitars (continued)

Guitar 2

Track 114 (only guitar 2)   Track 115 (both guitars)

Capo on 7th fret
All chords and tablature relative to capo

I was stand-ing at my win-dow on one cold and dis-mal day when I saw that hearse come roll-ing for to take my moth-er a-

Playing with a Slide

In Africa and India, the use of a "slide" on a stringed instrument to produce notes has been going on for ages.

Slides

The steel strings of the guitar make it a perfect match for using slides of various materials.

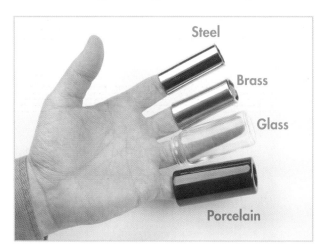

Steel

Brass

Glass

Porcelain

Besides being a lot of fun, playing slide guitar is also great for reinforcing your knowledge of chord shapes up and down the neck. When the slide is across any given fret (and be certain to line it up directly over the metal fret), playing only the D, G, and B strings will give you a major chord while playing only the G, B, and high E strings produces a minor chord.

Using a Slide

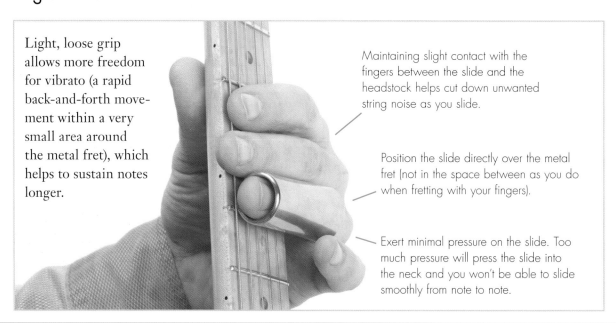

Light, loose grip allows more freedom for vibrato (a rapid back-and-forth movement within a very small area around the metal fret), which helps to sustain notes longer.

Maintaining slight contact with the fingers between the slide and the headstock helps cut down unwanted string noise as you slide.

Position the slide directly over the metal fret (not in the space between as you do when fretting with your fingers).

Exert minimal pressure on the slide. Too much pressure will press the slide into the neck and you won't be able to slide smoothly from note to note.

Here are some easy slide riffs you can play.

Alternate Tuning

Alternate tunings are created when you tune the strings of your guitar to notes other than those of standard tuning. Alternate tunings fall into three categories: lowered tunings, open tunings (which you'll learn about in upcoming pages), and alternate tunings.

In lowered tunings, your strings are tuned to the same intervals as in standard tuning, but set at lower pitches. Lowered tunings are used a lot in rock and metal music styles.

Standard Tuning:	E	A	D	G	B	E
E♭ Standard:	E♭	A♭	D♭	G♭	B♭	E♭
D Standard:	D	G	C	F	A	D
C♯ Standard:	C♯	F♯	B	E	G♯	C♯
C Standard:	C	F	B♭	E♭	G	C

Try to tune down from standard whenever possible in alternate tunings. Raising the pitch on too many strings, particularly the G, D, A, and low E, can put a lot of stress on the neck of your guitar.

In an alternate tuning, any one string (or up to all six) is changed from standard. Two very common alternate tunings are "Drop D," where just the low E string is tuned down a whole step to D, and "DADGAD" where both E strings are tuned down a whole step to D and the B string is also dropped a whole step to A. These two tunings are frequently used in Celtic and folk music.

Alternate tunings don't usually have names, per se, but go instead by the acronym of the retuned strings, listed from low (sixth string) to high (first string). Here are a few of the many possibilities:

E A D G B D	D A D D A D	C G D G A D	E B B G B D —
E A D G C F	D A D G B D	C G D G B E	Ani DiFranco uses
E A D G♯ B E	D A C♯ F♯ A D	C G D G B D	this in *Not a Pretty*
E A D E A D	D G D G A D	C G D G C D	*Girl*. Both the
E A D F♯ B E	D G D G B E	C F C G C E	fourth and fifth
E B D G A D	D G D F♯ B D	C F C F A D	strings are tuned to
E B E G A D	C A D G B E		the same note.

Since Drop D and DADGAD are two commonly used alternate tunings, here are a few exercises in each to help you get started exploring this aspect of playing guitar:

Guitar in Drop D tuning
Low to high: D A D G B E

Track 117

Guitar in DADGAD tuning
Low to high: D A D G A D

Track 118

Practice: Double Drop D Tuning

Here is an arrangement of the traditional song, "Man of Constant Sorrow," that makes great use of Double Drop D tuning. Pay particular attention to the shift in position when you play the G chords.

Track 119

Practice: Celtic Song in DADGAD Tuning

"Carrickfergus" is another old Irish song that has been covered by many artists, including Van Morrison, Joan Baez, and Bryan Ferry. This simple fingerstyle arrangement is done in DADGAD tuning.

Track 120

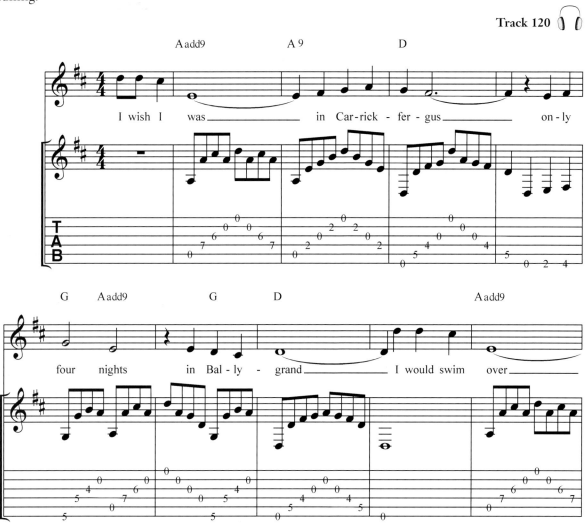

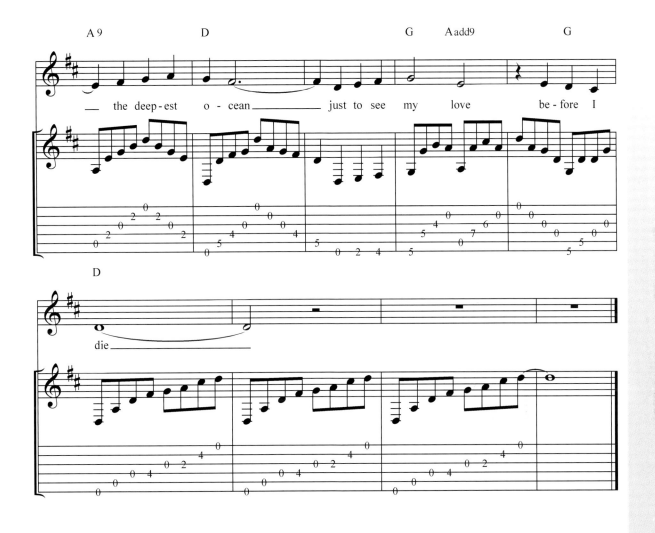

Alternate tunings are used on all types of guitars, whether acoustic, electric, or classical, but you should *not* use alternate tunings if you have an electric guitar with a floating tremolo system (a whammy bar that both lowers and raises the pitch of the strings). Unless you can lock the tremolo system into place, you'll find it almost impossible to keep your guitar in tune if you try any tuning other than standard.

Practice: Song in Unusual Alternate Tuning

To further explore the many possibilities of alternate tuning, here is an original "Lullaby" written in CGDGCD tuning.

Track 121 🎧

Open Tuning

In an *open tuning*, the strings of the guitar are tuned to the notes of a specific, recognizable chord, such as G, A, E, D, C, F, Gm, Em, Gma7, and so on.

When you strum an open-tuned guitar, you get the chord made up of the notes that the strings are tuned to. Strum a guitar tuned to open G and you get a G chord. This also means that barring all the strings at any fret will produce a chord as well. If you're in open G tuning, barring the second fret will produce an A chord. Barring the fifth fret will be a C chord.

Here are some of the most common open tunings:

Standard Tuning:	E	A	D	G	B	E
Open G Tuning:	D	G	D	G	B	D
Open G Tuning: (variation)	G	B	D	G	B	D
Open D Tuning:	D	A	D	F♯	A	D
Open A Tuning:	E	A	E	A	C♯	E
Open E Tuning:	E	B	E	G♯	B	E
Open C Tuning:	C	G	C	G	C	E
Open C Tuning: (variation)	C	G	C	E	G	C
Open F Tuning:	C	F	C	F	A	C

You can also use a capo to raise the pitch of any alternate or open tuning. If you tune to open D and place a capo on the second fret, you've just placed yourself in open E tuning.

To give you a taste of open tunings, here is a very simple exercise (which, as a bonus, sounds like a song) played in Cmaj7 tuning (low to high: CGDGBE)

Guitar in open Cmaj7 tuning
Low to high: C G C G B E

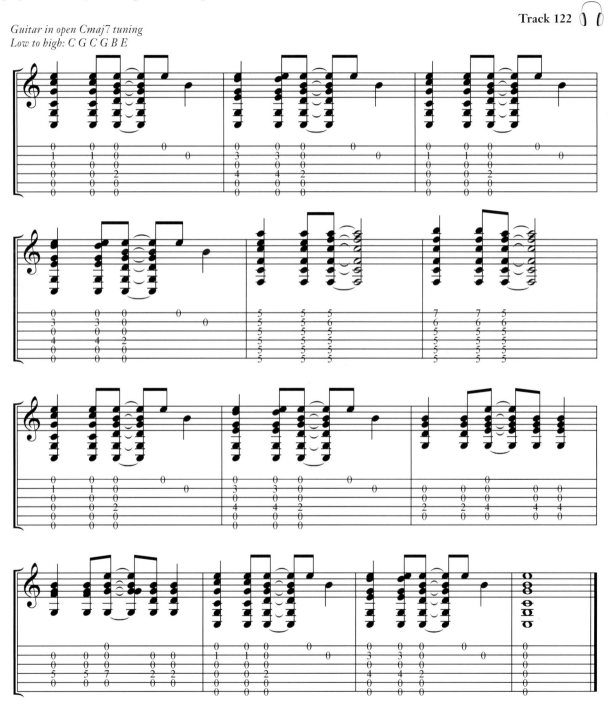

Practice: Open G Tuning

To help you get acquainted with open G tuning, here are some exercises. This first set focuses on strumming and chord changes, making use of an open position Am7 shape:

Track 123

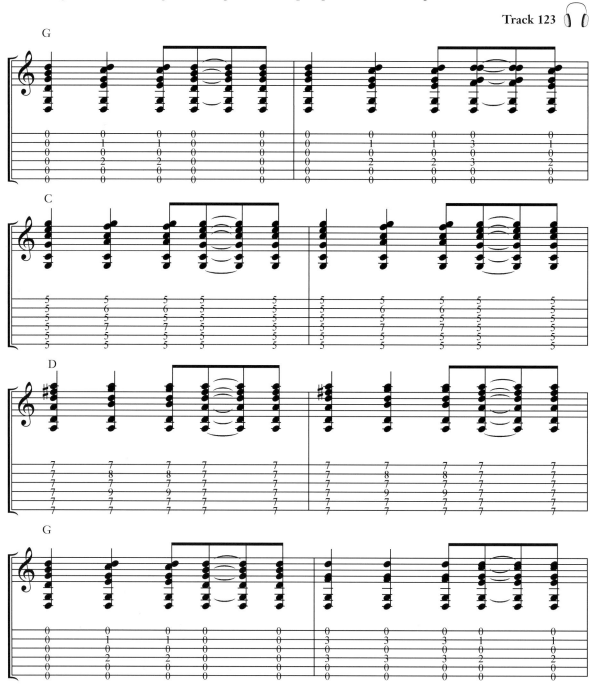

Fingerpicking in open G tuning is part of the beautiful sound of Hawaiian slack-key guitar playing. These exercises will give you some practice to prepare for the upcoming slack-key style song you'll be learning.

Track 124

Practice: Rock Song in Open G Tuning

When Bruce Springsteen released his 2006 album *We Shall Overcome: The Seeger Sessions*, "Pay Me My Money Down" was the first single. This arrangement, done in open G tuning, also draws a lot of inspiration from Keith Richards' guitar playing.

Track 125

Guitar in Open G tuning.
From low to high: D G D G B D

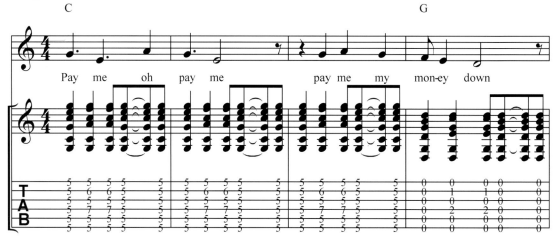

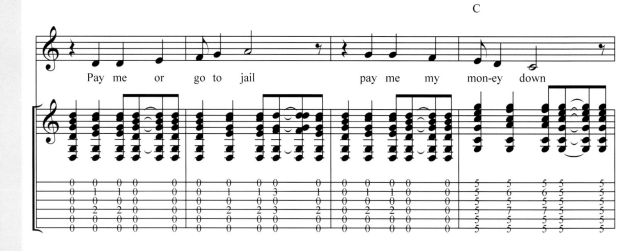

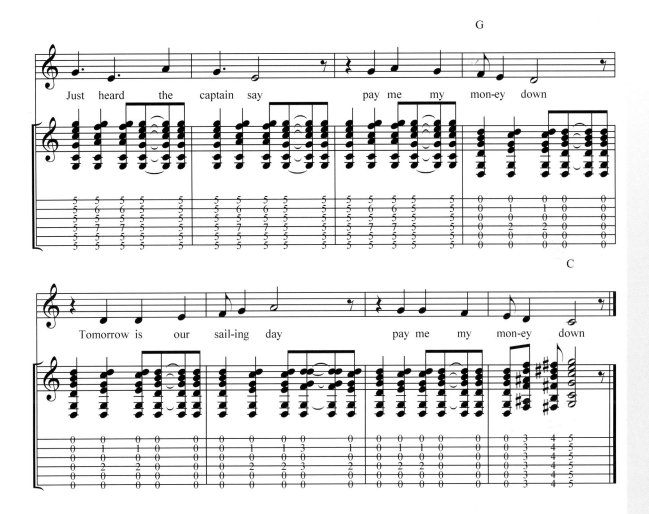

Practice: Hawaiian Slack-key Style in Open G Tuning

"Kī Hōʻalu" is an instrumental written in the style of Hawaiian "slack key" guitarists. It's played in open G (known as "Taro Patch" tuning in the Aloha State) and uses a steady alternating bass to accompany the syncopated melody.

Track 126

Practice: Open D Tuning

Here are some exercises in open D tuning that focus on fingerpicking.

Track 127

Open tunings are often used by slide guitar players. Here are some slide exercises in open D.

Practice: Fingerstyle in Open D Tuning

This open D arrangement of "Buffalo Gals" uses a walking bass line on the A string. Take time to familiarize yourself with the chord shapes, which will be slightly different than what you're used to in standard tuning.

Track 129

Practice: Blues Song in Open D Tuning with Slide

Open tunings, slide guitar, and the blues are a perfect combination. In "Empty Bed Blues" you play all the notes on the neck with a slide (except those of the open strings). If you don't have a slide you can just fret the notes regularly.

Track 130

Crosspicking

Crosspicking is a picking technique that allows you to mimic fast fingerpicking with a pick instead of your fingers. It was first developed by bluegrass mandolin players like Jesse McReynolds and subsequently picked up by guitarists like George Shuffler and Doc Watson.

Different Picking Options

The secret to crosspicking is to know which way to pick the strings most efficiently for the music at hand. Typically, a guitarist will pick in one of three ways:

- **Unidirectional**—picking in one direction (usually in downstrokes).

- **Alternate**—picking in regularly alternating downstrokes and upstrokes.

- **Economy** (or **convenience**)—picking in the direction of the next string to be played.

Try all three picking styles in this example:

unidirectional picking (all downstokes)   *alternate picking*   *economy (convenience) picking*

Once you get used to it, you'll probably find economy picking to be the most efficient for this particular musical phrase.

> You want to be comfortable with each type of picking. Good guitarists let the music decide which style of picking to use. Unidirectional, using all downstrokes, is great for palm muting, as well as driving rock and punk rhythms. Many reggae rhythms involve only upstrokes. Alternate picking suits most basic strumming and single-note lead playing. Economy picking gives you rolling syncopated single notes at fast tempos.

Here are some simple exercises to help you get acquainted with the crosspicking technique. Be sure to pay close attention to the picking direction symbols:

Practice: Focusing on Crosspicking

You'll hear lots of crosspicking used in bluegrass music, but it's a technique used in almost all musical genres. This arrangement of "She'll Be Comin' 'Round the Mountain" is done in a crosspicked style similar to songs like Green Day's "Good Riddance (Time of Your Life)."

Creating Fills

Music breathes. The rhythm of every song includes spaces where the singing takes a break for a moment and other instruments step in to fill the gap. The guitar is tailor-made to provide *fills*, short melodic phrases, during a song—even when the song is played by a single guitarist.

The tricky part of adding fills to your playing is to smoothly switch from playing chords to playing single notes, and then switch back again. This is where your knowledge of keys, major scales, and chords can help.

Suppose you're playing a song in the key of G. You already know the G major scale. Knowing the G major pentatonic scale, which only has five different notes, can be an even bigger help:

G Major Pentatonic Scale

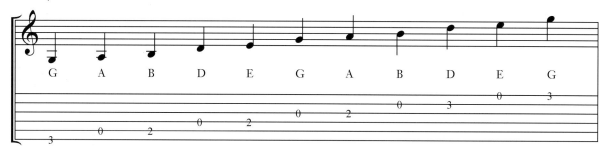

Notice how many notes of the G major pentatonic involve open strings. This allows you to make quick use of hammer-ons and pull-offs and still get back to your next chord on time.

You usually don't get much time for a fill (two to four beats is typical) so practice playing a chord for four beats, switching to a fill—even if it's just one or two notes—and then returning to the chord:

Track 133

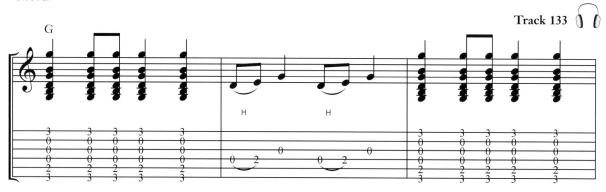

The fills in your upcoming song, "O Susannah," will look somewhat difficult at first. But if you examine them individually and work them out slowly, you'll find that they're simply hammer-ons, pull-offs, and slides you've done before. Master these exercises and you'll be ready for the practice song.

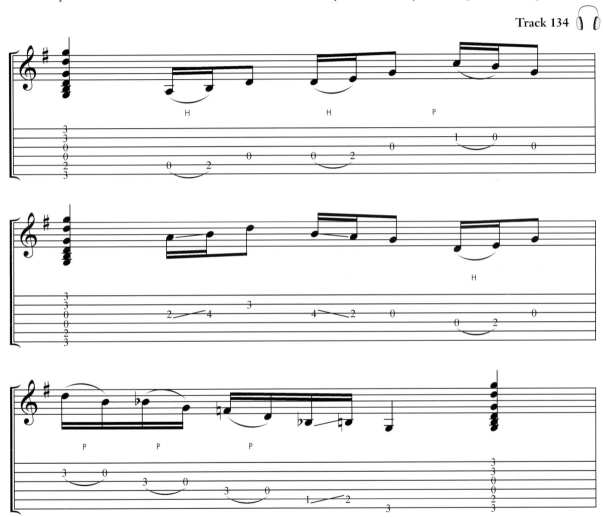

Track 134

Practice: Fills Within a Song

This arrangement of "O Susannah," played in the style of songs like "Sweet Home Alabama," is chock-full of fills. You'll get a lot of practice on your hammer-ons, pull-offs, and slides.

Track 135

Chord Melody

Songs have three components: melody, harmony, and rhythm. Your guitar playing up to now has focused on learning chords (harmony) and strumming (rhythm). Aside from singing along with a song, you probably haven't given much thought to melody. But your guitar can be a whole band when you want it to be. In addition to harmony and strumming, you've also added the occasional bass line or two. The technique of *chord melody* focuses on the melody, adding it to the harmony and rhythms, and allowing you to explore even more of your guitar's potential.

To get you started on this technique, here's a melody you should immediately recognize:

Ideally you want to play your melody on the high E, B, and G strings in order to bring it out over the accompanying chords. Speaking of which, here are the chords for this snippet of "Ode to Joy" which, for this example, is in the key of A major:

As you'll discover, there are many ways to create a chord melody. Start as simply as possible, strumming the accompanying chord only on the first beat of each measure and making certain to strum only to the string of the melody note:

Track 136

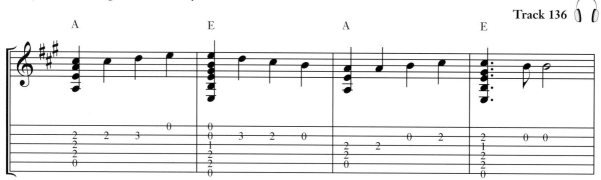

You probably noticed that you had to add the C♯ note at the second fret of the B string to your E chord to make it work. The notes of any melody aren't always the notes of the accompanying chord, so you occasionally will be adding additional notes to your chords.

Try the "Ode to Joy" melody again, this time strumming chords on the first and third beats:

Track 137

You can definitely hear how the melody creates changes in the chords. The D note over the second A chord in the first measure turns the A into Asus4. Likewise, the open B string played with the A in the third measure creates an Asus2.

Chord melody works exceptionally well with fingerpicking. Playing even two notes at a time can imply a fuller harmony than you're actually playing. Here is a simple picking pattern for the "Ode to Joy" melody:

Track 138

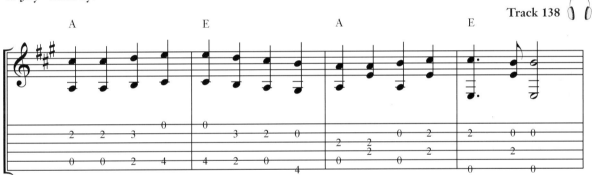

Finally, try something slightly more challenging:

Track 139

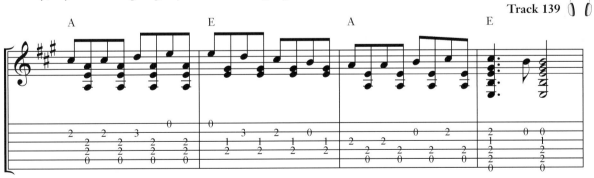

As with everything you've learned so far, chord melody takes practice and patience, but you should find it a very rich and rewarding technique.

Practice: Simple Chord Melody

You can't go wrong using "Brahms' Lullaby" as your first try at playing chord melody. This arrangement uses simple variations of the basic G, D, and C chords. Be sure to strum only the necessary strings and to emphasize the melody.

Track 140

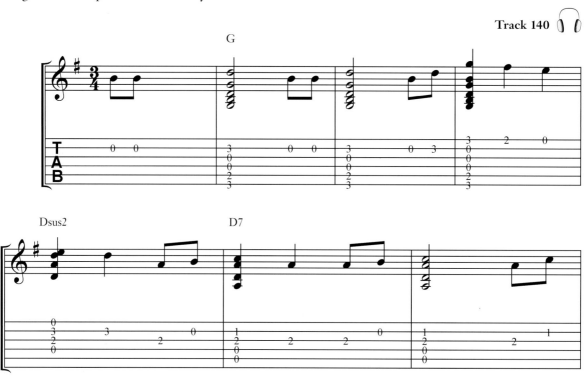

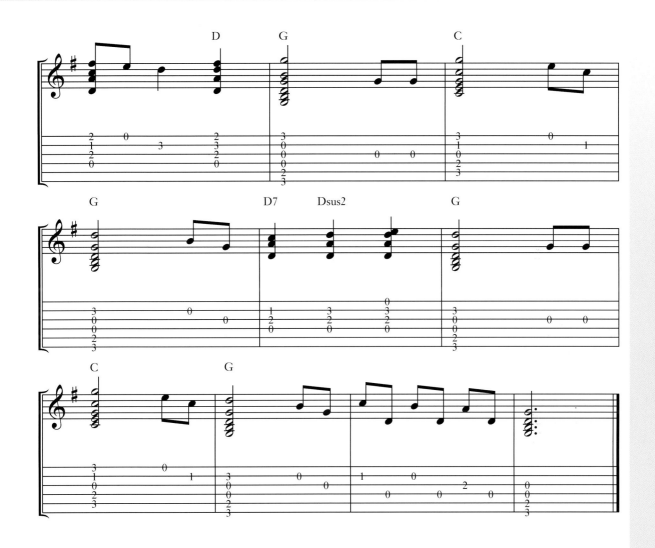

Getting Fancy with Chord Melody

As you learn more about the guitar and about music, you can use that knowledge to make your chord melody playing even fancier. Taking advantage of drop D tuning, for example, as well as using the notes of the open strings to allow you to shift from one place to another on the neck, can lead to more interesting arrangements:

Track 141

Guitar in Drop D tuning
Low to high: D A D G B E

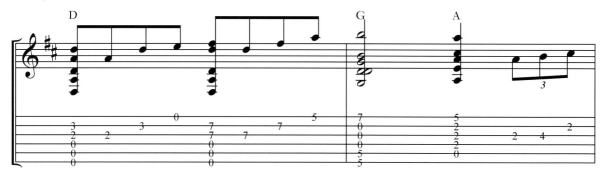

You can also take advantage of the various chord voicings you know up and down the neck of the guitar, combined with a bit of "pinch" picking:

Track 142

Guitar in Drop D tuning
Low to high: D A D G B E

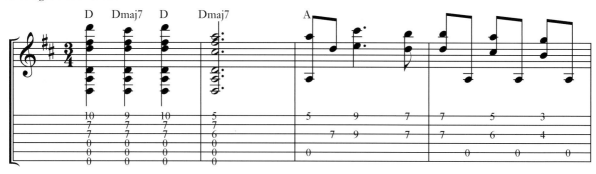

Creating your own chord melody arrangements of songs is easy in that you can go at your own pace. Start out with very simple arrangements of very simple melodies and then work your way up as your guitar skills and musical knowledge grow and evolve.

To get you started spicing up your chord melody technique, try this arrangement of the traditional Irish tune "Tom O'Hara."

Track 143

Practice: Fancy Chord Melody

A song as lovely as "Beautiful Dreamer" deserves a beautiful arrangement. This one incorporates drop D tuning, fancy chord voicings, and occasional Travis pinching to create an enchanting rendition of this Stephen Foster classic. It's also deceptively easy to play.

Track 144

Guitar in Drop D tuning
Low to high: D A D G B E

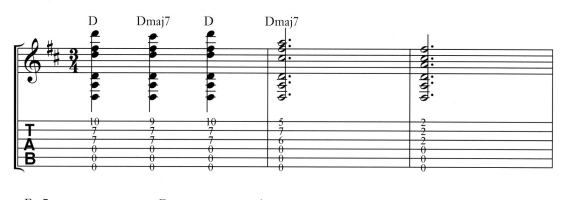

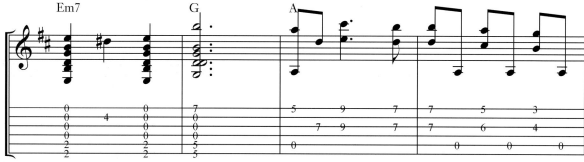

Playing in a Group

Playing music with others is even more fun than playing on your own. More important, it's a terrific way to learn more about the guitar and music in general. Musicians love to share tips to help others improve their knowledge and skills. You should play with other guitarists and musicians every chance you get.

Initially, you'll be thrilled to be strumming along with everyone, changing chords and keeping the rhythm steady and true. As you gain confidence in your abilities, you'll want to try out playing different parts (much as you did when you learned how to use a capo earlier) to bring more depth and musical texture to the overall sound.

A Few Tips

Whenever possible, try to know the basics of any given song you're playing. If you have to constantly watch a piece of paper or the screen of a tablet, you'll spend less time interacting with your fellow musicians.

If someone else is handling the primary strumming, use both your knowledge and your ears to create a second guitar part that complements the song you're playing. If someone's doing a steady strum, try arpeggios. If someone's doing a complicated fingerpicking pattern, use sparse chords, preferably on a different area of the neck of the guitar.

The more people playing, the more important it is to play less and to listen. A musician's ears are his greatest asset, and playing with others is probably the best way to develop yours.

Here is the first guitar part for "Saint James Infirmary." It's simple and sparse, and you should get comfortable with it before trying out the second guitar part.

Track 145

Practice: Playing in a Group—Second Guitar

This second guitar part for "Saint James Infirmary" involves most of the various techniques you've learned. Take your time and study it phrase by phrase. Then play along with either the second guitar or both guitar parts. When you're ready, try playing along with just the first guitar part. You'll hopefully be impressed with your progress as a guitarist.

Glossary

accidental   A sharp sign, flat sign, or natural sign.

acoustic guitar   Technically, any non-amplified guitar. However, it has become customary for the term "acoustic" to refer to flat-top steel-string guitars, as opposed to classical guitars.

alternate picking   Picking single notes in a continual down-and-up motion.

alternate tuning   Tuning the strings of the guitar to notes other than those of standard tuning.

alternating bass   A strum played like the "bass/strum" but with the root note in the bass note played on the first beat only and another note (usually the fifth of the chord) played on the third beat.

arpeggio   A chord played one note at a time (usually on separate strings), most often in an ascending or descending order.

augmented chord   One of the four basic chord types, made up of the root, major third, and augmented fifth degrees of the major scale.

bar   Also called a "measure;" a distinct measurement of beats, dictated by the time signature. The end of a bar is indicated by a vertical line running through the staff or bass guitar tablature lines.

barre chords   Chords that are formed by placing the index finger flat across the strings at a single fret to play some notes while the other fingers fret others higher up on the neck. Fretting across all six strings is called a "full barre" and fretting between two and five strings is called a "half barre."

bass/strum   A strumming pattern created by playing the root note of a chord in the bass on the first and third beats and the rest of the chord on the other strings on the second and fourth beats.

bend   A guitar slur technique, pushing a string along the fingerboard toward the center of the neck to raise its pitch from one note to that of another note.

bridge   The part of the body of the guitar where the strings are anchored to the body.

capo   A clamp device attached to the neck and fingerboard to equally raise the pitch of all strings.

chord   Three or more different notes played together at the same time.

chord chart   A diagram that shows where to place your fingers to play a specific chord.

chord progression   A sequence of chords played in a song or in a phrase of a song.

chromatic scale   A scale made up of all 12 possible notes, each one a half-step from another.

Circle of Fifths   A pattern that can be used to study the relationship of keys to one another; also an excellent tool for practicing scales, riffs, or phrases in all keys.

classical guitar   A guitar with nylon strings, usually slightly smaller than the typical acoustic guitar.

crosspicking   A method of playing guitar with a pick where the guitarist uses a steady stream of single notes, usually played across three or four strings.

DADGAD tuning   A popular alternate tuning where the six strings of the guitar are tuned, low to high, to D, A, D, G, A, and D. This tuning is often used in Celtic music.

diatonic   The notes used in a given major scale or the chords derived from the triads of that scale.

diminished chord   One of the four basic chord types, made up of the root, minor third, and diminished fifth degrees of the major scale.

dotted note   A dot added to a note in order to give it more length; a dotted half note is three beats long; a dotted quarter note is one and a half beats long, and so on.

Double Drop D tuning   An alternate tuning in which both the low and high E strings are tuned down a whole step to D.

double stops   Simultaneously playing two notes on adjacent strings.

dreadnought   An acoustic guitar body shape with a boxier and deeper body and bolder tone than a typical classical guitar.

Drop D tuning   An alternate tuning in which the low E string is tuned down a whole step to D.

economy picking   Picking in the direction of the next string to be struck.

eighth note   A note of half a beat's duration.

eighth note rest   A rest of half a beat's duration.

electric guitar   A guitar requiring amplification to be heard. Most electric guitars have solid bodies, but there are hollow body and semi-hollow body electric guitars as well.

fill   A short musical phrase that fills a space in the music. Similar to riffs except that riffs are usually repeated note by note while fills usually are different each time.

fingerpicking   A style of playing that uses the fingers instead of a pick to strike the strings.

flat   An accidental sign indicating lowering a note a half-step.

fret   Metal wire on the neck of the guitar; also the act of placing one's finger on the neck.

fretboard   The area along the front of the guitar's neck where one places the fingers to fret notes on the strings.

grace note   A note played and then changed to another note within the shortest time possible.

half note   A note of two beats' duration.

half rest   A rest of two beats' duration.

half-step   The difference, between two notes, of one fret on the neck of the guitar.

hammer-on   A left-hand slurring technique in which a second note is sounded by the addition of a finger.

interval   The distance, in terms of steps and half-steps, of one note from another.

key   The tonal center of a piece of music.

key signature   The number of flats or sharps (if any) used in a song, which usually indicates the key the song is in.

major chord   One of the four basic chord types, made up of the root, major third, and perfect fifth degrees of the major scale.

major scale   The basic building block of music theory, the major scale begins on any note and uses the following sequence:

root—whole step—whole step—half-step—whole step—whole step—whole step—half-step (the root again)

measure   Also called a "bar;" a measurement of beats, dictated by the time signature. The end of a measure is indicated by a vertical line running through the staff or bass guitar tablature lines.

minor chord   One of the four basic chord types, made up of the root, minor third, and perfect fifth degrees of the major scale.

music notation   A system for reading music using a staff and notes placed upon it; the location of the note on the staff determines its name, and the type of note indicates its duration.

natural sign   An accidental sign indicating to play a note with neither flats nor sharps.

note   A musical tone of a specific pitch.

nut   A notched strip of hard plastic, bone, or other material located between the neck and the headstock on the guitar's fingerboard.

octave   An interval of eight named notes from the root note, bearing the same name as the root note.

open tuning   Tuning the strings of the guitar so that they create an easily identifiable chord when strummed without any stings being fretted. For example, strumming the open strings of a guitar tuned to open G tuning will sound a G major chord.

pick   Also called "plectrum," a hard, flat piece of material (usually plastic) used to strike the strings instead of a finger of the right hand.

pinch   A fingerpicking technique where two notes are played simultaneously by the right hand by picking the lower one with the thumb and the higher one with a finger.

pull-off   A left hand slurring technique in which a second note is sounded by removal of a finger.

quarter note   A note of one beat's duration.

quarter rest   A rest of one beat's duration.

root note   The note named by a chord; "C" is the root note of a C major chord.

saddle   The raised area on the guitar's bridge, usually made of hard plastic, bone, or other material on acoustic and classical guitars.

sharp   An accidental sign indicating raising a note a half-step.

sixteenth note   A note of one quarter of a beat's duration.

sixteenth rest   A rest of one quarter of a beat's duration.

slash shord   A chord that uses a note other than its root note as a bass note. It's written with a "/"; "C/B" is a C major chord played with a B note (not a usual note of the C chord) as the bass note.

slide   A left hand slurring technique involving sliding a finger from one fret to another. A slide is also a cylinder of glass, metal, or porcelain used instead of fingers to fret the notes along the neck.

slur   Using a left hand technique to articulate a note or series of notes.

staff   A set of five lines, used in music notation to indicate note names.

standard tuning   The way the strings of a guitar are usually tuned, from low to high: E, A, D, G, B, and E.

Glossary (continued)

step   The difference, between two notes, of two frets on the neck of the guitar.

straight eighths   Eighth notes played as even eighth notes; that is, dividing the beat in half.

swing eighths   Playing eighth notes as the first and last of a set of triplets (as opposed to "straight eighths").

syncopation   Notes that fall on the offbeats.

tablature   A system of reading music involving six horizontal lines (indicating the strings of the guitar) and numbers (indicating which frets to play in order to sound the notes).

tie   An arced line connecting two notes of the same pitch, adding the time value of the second note to the first; a whole note tied to a half note will last for six beats.

time signature   Usually indicated by a fraction at the start of a piece of music (for example, $\frac{3}{4}$), the time signature will tell you how many beats each measure receives (the upper number of the fraction) and which type of note is designated as a single beat (the lower number).

transposing   Changing the notes (and chords) of a song from one key to another.

triplet   A note of one third of a beat's duration.

whole note   A note of four beats' duration.

whole note rest   A rest of four beats' duration.

Chord Charts

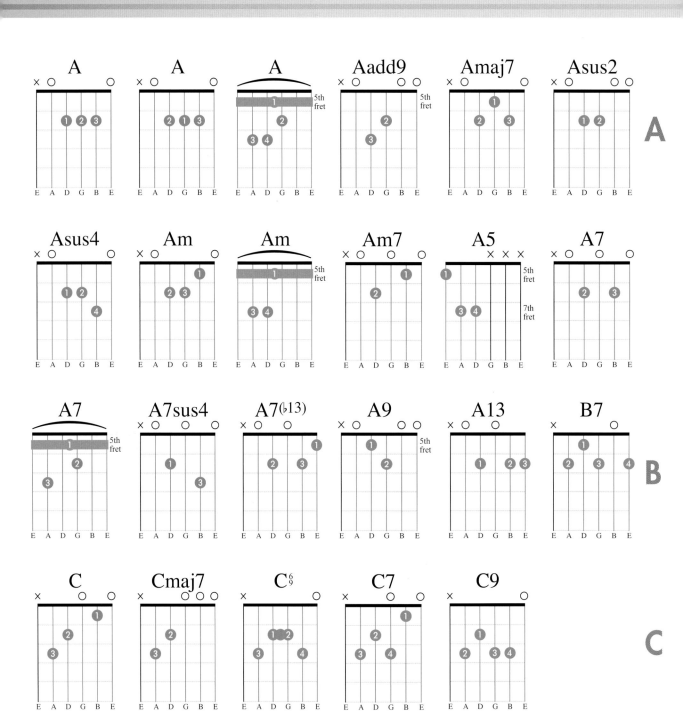

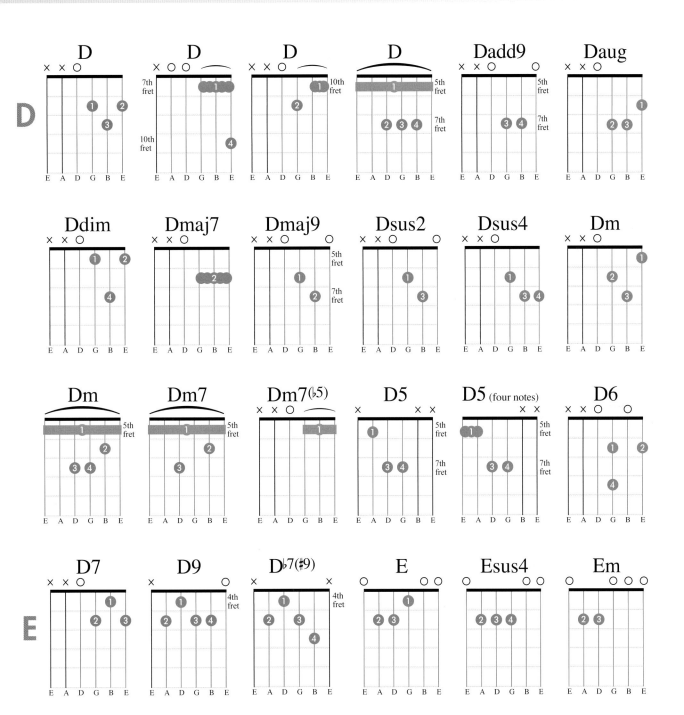

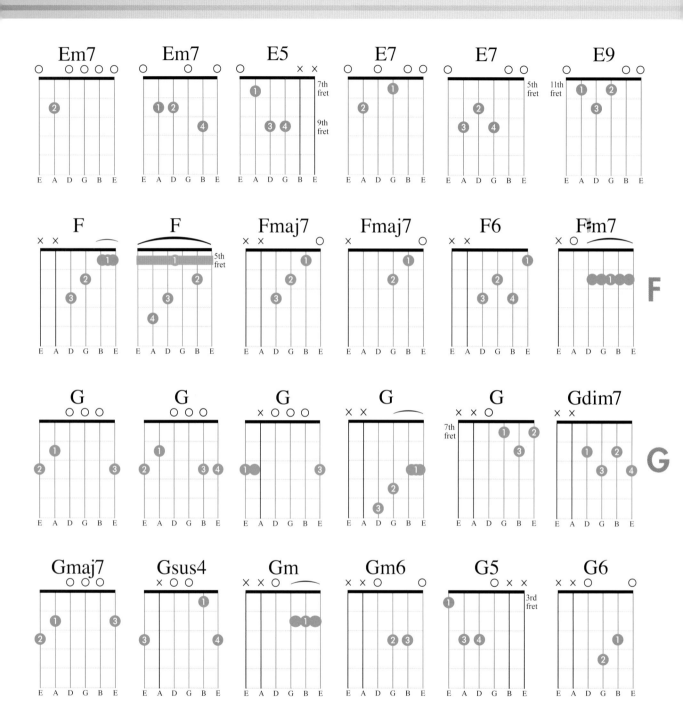

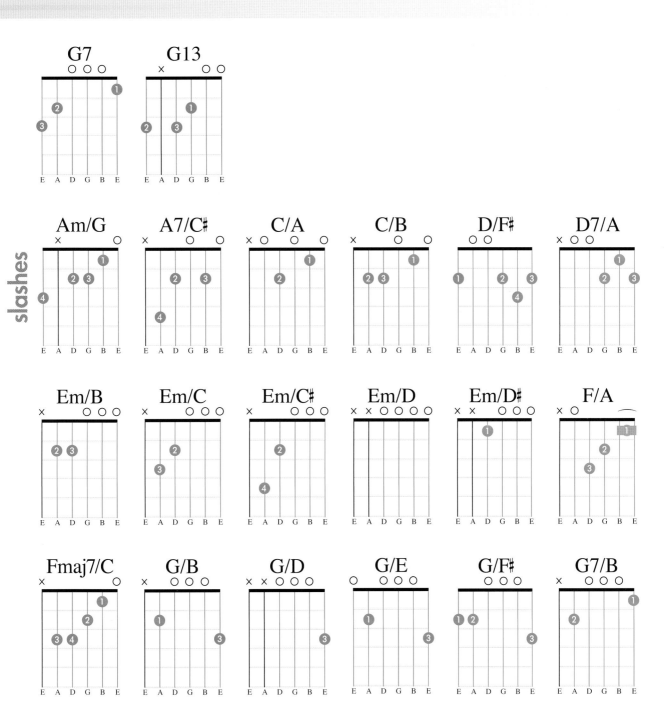

For Further Study

Now that you've taken more than a few "first steps" with your guitar, you'll undoubtedly want to continue learning and growing. There are many possible musical roads to explore and, fortunately, thousands of books, videos, and CD and DVD tutorials, not to mention all the various tutorial websites on the internet, to help you.

Andrew DuBrock's *Total Acoustic Guitar* (Hal Leonard, 2010) gives you a great review of the basics while working through the early intermediate stages of playing.

You'll also find that *Acoustic Guitar* (not just the magazine, but also their exceptional website, which contains an amazing archive of guitar tutorials) can help you with just about any of your guitar questions. Also be sure to check out their books, such as *Rhythm Guitar Essentials* (String Letter Publishing, 2009) and *Flatpicking Guitar Basics* (String Letter Publishing, 2010) for even more helpful lessons.

Hemme Luttjeboer's *The Complete Idiot's Guide to Guitar Exercises* (Alpha, 2010) gives you an extensive range of drills, from warmups and basic techniques to dexterity- and stamina-building exercises. You'll also get to work on single-note scales, chord exercises, and fingerpicking.

Practicing is an essential part of improving as a guitarist, and you can help yourself put both your mind and body at their best by reading *The Musician's Way: A Guide to Practice, Performance, and Wellness* by Gerald Klickstein (Oxford University Press, 2009) and Jamie Andreas' *The Principles of Correct Practice for Guitar, Second Edition* (Jamey World, Inc., 2005). Both of these books will give you the mindset you need to make the most of your practice and to become the best guitarist you possibly can.

If you'd like more material on music theory, I highly recommend both Michael Miller's *The Complete Idiot's Guide to Music Theory* (Alpha Books, 2002) and *Music Theory for Guitarists*, by Tom Serb (Noteboat, Inc., 2003).

Mark Hansen's *The Complete Book of Alternate Tunings* (Music Sales America, 1995), is a great introduction to nonstandard tunings.

For more work on fills and a great introduction to blues guitar basics, John Ganapes' *Blues You Can Use* (Hal Leonard, 1995) and any of Dave Rubin's "Inside the Blues" tutorial books, like *12-Bar Blues* (Hal Leonard, 1999), are excellent choices.

Even with all the books, DVDs, and websites available, you might want to think about getting a teacher, either for private lessons or as part of a group class. When you're starting out, a teacher can provide instant feedback and help you avoid snags that beginners typically deal with.

And as good as one-on-one instruction is, you'll learn even more whenever you play along with others.

And please feel free to write and ask me any questions, too. My email address is dhodgeguitar@aol.com. You can also reach me at Guitar Noise—www.guitarnoise.com (a wonderful free guitar tutorial website, by the way). I try to answer every email I get, but I do spend my days teaching, so please don't worry if I don't respond immediately.

You have a lifetime of making music ahead of you. Play every chance you get and, above all, have fun!

Index

Index (continued)

V

W

Photo Credits

All music notation by David Hodge using Finale software by MakeMusic, Inc.
All line art by Laura Robbins, Pearson Technology Group, and Brian Massey, Alpha Books.

Ogden Gigli:
7, 16, 18, 24, 26-27, 30, 32, 36, 39-43, 65, 86-87, 102, 104-105, 110-111, 118, 122, 132-133, 138-139, 150-151, 154, 158-159, 162-165, 168-169, 176, 182, 234

1		Matthew Ward © Dorling Kindersley
2		courtesy of Karen Berger
4	left	courtesy of Karen Berger
	right	Gary Ombler © Dorling Kindersley, courtesy of *Classical Guitar* magazine
5	left	Gary Ombler © Dorling Kindersley, courtesy of The National Music Museum
	center	Gary Ombler © Dorling Kindersley
	right	Nick Harris © Dorling Kindersley
6		Nick Harris © Dorling Kindersley
8	left	Gary Ombler © Dorling Kindersley
9	left	Nick Harris © Dorling Kindersley
10		Nick Harris © Dorling Kindersley
11	top	Gary Ombler © Dorling Kindersley
11	center	Nick Harris © Dorling Kindersley
11	bottom	Nick Harris © Dorling Kindersley
12		Garth Blore © Dorling Kindersley
13		Nick Harris © Dorling Kindersley
15		© Dorling Kindersley
17		© Dorling Kindersley
20-21		© Dorling Kindersley
22	middle	Ogden Gigli
22	bottom	Geoff Dann © Dorling Kindersley
25	top 2	Ogden Gigli
25	bottom	Matthew Ward © Dorling Kindersley
28	top	Andy Crawford © Dorling Kindersley
28	bottom 2	Ogden Gigli
29	right	Ogden Gigli
29	bottom	Andy Crawford © Dorling Kindersley
31		Andy Crawford © Dorling Kindersley
222		courtesy of John Reichert
223		Gary Ombler © Dorling Kindersley
231		Roger d'Olivere Mapp © Rough Guides
245		Gareth Boden, Pearson Education Ltd.
246-247		Alessandra Santarelli and Joeff Davis © Dorling Kindersley